THE POLICY MACHINE

The Department of State and American Foreign Policy

THE
POLICY
MACHINE

The Department of State and American Foreign Policy

Robert Ellsworth Elder

SYRACUSE UNIVERSITY PRESS 1960

JX1705
E4

This work has been published
with the assistance of a
FORD FOUNDATION GRANT

Preface

Americans normally know the Department of State—if at all—
through its voice, the rather abstract policy declarations which ema-
nate from it in endless stream, without understanding the Department's
flesh and bones, its organization, processes, and personnel in a government-wide setting. Attempting to make the policy-making procedures
and related problems of such a complicated mechanism as the Department "come alive" for the lay reader or student—members of what
Gabriel Almond has called the "attentive public"—has been a challenging task. I am still not certain that it has been or can be accomplished
successfully.

No individual or research group can "catch" the Department and
portray or analyze it in down-to-earth, human terms on a single day,
yet its parts are continuously changing names or modifying their relationships to each other. Fortunately, certain basic elements of the
policy-making process remain a bit more constant. It is some of these
essential parts of the whole which have been selected for description
and analysis. If there remains a plethora of detail, a portion of which
is likely to be outdated in time, its inclusion was deemed necessary.
The Department officer who is perhaps most knowledgeable in the field
of study covered by the book occasionally lectures middle-grade officer
groups at the Foreign Service Institute with the following admonition:
"Be sure you pave the road to your conclusions with as much solid
fact as possible and avoid the running broad-jump approach." I have
tried to heed this excellent advice.

I do apologize for making only passing mention of certain organizational elements of the Department which are of considerable importance, such as the Bureaus of International Organization Affairs and
Economic Affairs. And, I would have liked to say more about the role
of higher-ranking officers in the Department from the Assistant Secre-

tary level on up and concerning relationships with the Department of Defense and other agencies of the executive branch. Limitations upon time for research and writing precluded complete coverage, but I have sought to focus clearly upon those elements of the Department which were included for discussion.

The men under whom I studied as a graduate student in international relations at the University of Chicago set much of the intellectual framework within which my study of the Department was conducted. Among these professors who provided inspiration by their own teaching, research, and writing were Quincy Wright, J. Fred Rippy, T. V. Smith, Harold Lasswell, Nathan Leites, Bernadotte Schmitt, Pitman Potter, Wellington Jones, Henry Leppard, and Charles Colby.

At Colgate University, I owe a lasting debt to Professor Paul Jacobsen, Chairman of the Department of Political Science (who reintroduced me to Washington during the spring of 1952 in the last of his thirteen years in the job I was to take over), and Professor Rodney Mott, Director of the Division of the Social Sciences. They have allowed me to serve as Director of the Colgate-Washington Study Group since 1952, a post which has made it possible for me to spend nine spring semesters in the nation's Capital and to conduct over 750 group interviews (of which some two hundred were in the Department of State) with leaders in all branches of the government.

The Ford Foundation's Fund for the Advancement of Education provided me with the means of studying staffwork with the Committee on Foreign Relations of the United States Senate and in the Foreign Affairs and Senior Specialists Divisions of the Legislative Reference Service during the fall semester of 1955, and in the Department of State during the fall semester of 1956. Although much of the congressional part of the experience was on an internship basis, the more than one hundred formally recorded individual interviews conducted in 1955 and 1956 provided the core of material from which the basic draft of the book was first prepared during the spring of 1958. Of course, I was also able to draw on past and current interviews of the Study Group to supplement the interviews and experiences under the grant.

The opportunity to participate in The Brookings Institution's study on the formulation and administration of foreign policy for the Committee on Foreign Relations during the spring and summer of 1959— while it postponed publication of the book by a year—broadened my knowledge of the government-wide process of policy-making in the foreign affairs field, gave me a chance to re-explore the Department in depth through some eighty interviews, and permitted me to gather material from which the final two chapters of the book have been written. The discussions by members of the staff working on the Brookings study and access to the suggestions of the distinguished advisory committee which reviewed staff drafts were substantively valuable and intellectually stimulating.

It is impossible to acknowledge by name the hundreds of people who have talked with me in the Department and elsewhere in government and whose ideas have been weighed and blended in the final product, but I do appreciate and thoroughly enjoyed the more than one thousand hours which they willingly devoted to telling me in formal interviews about their jobs and problems. A host of unscheduled informal conversations were also productive, sometimes more so than formal discussions, but I have kept no accounting of them.

I must give personal credit to five individuals whose cooperation and encouragement have been of special help. E. Taylor Parks of the Historical Office in the Department of State is known to thousands of researchers as their point of entry into the Department. His knowledge of the Department, past and present, is great. He not only took care of my practical needs during my period of study in the Department in 1956 but also has given me useful advice of both a substantive and procedural character at that time and since. Gwen Barrows, Managing Editor of the *Foreign Service Journal*, published several of my articles on the Department in the *Journal* and by her continued interest in my research encouraged me to put the material together in book form. H. Field Haviland, Jr., who directed the Brookings study, has contributed in large measure to the chapter on personnel management, not only by directing my attention to certain issues but also by judicious editing and the insertion of key sentences and phrases. However, he cannot be held accountable for the chapter as it appears in the book, because I have chosen to use my own final draft rather than the edited version published in the Brookings study. Although the emphasis in the book is on the Department of State, knowledge of staffwork in Congress was quite useful, and I must thank Carl Marcy, Chief of Staff for the Committee on Foreign Relations, and Ernest Griffith of American University, then Director of the Legislative Reference Service, for guiding my studies during the fall of 1955.

I am grateful to the editors of the *Foreign Service Journal* and the *Western Political Quarterly* for permission to incorporate in the book revisions of articles of mine which they had originally published. Included from the *Journal* are "Country Desk Officer: Low Man on the Totem Pole," May and June, 1958, and "Thank You, Mr. Secretary," August, 1957. From the *Quarterly*, I have used all of "The Public

Studies Division of the Department of State: Public Opinion Analysts in the Formulation and Conduct of American Foreign Policy," December, 1957, and significant portions of "Soviet-American Tension: A Reassessment," June, 1952, and "Factors Affecting Stability of the Balance of Power," June, 1950. In addition, I thank The Brookings Institution for permission to use my final draft on personnel management which appeared with some revision in "The Formulation and Administration of United States Foreign Policy" prepared by The Brookings Institution at the request of the Committee on Foreign Relations and published as a committee print on January 13, 1960 by the Government Printing Office in Washington, D.C.

I deeply appreciate the excellent editorial suggestions and intelligent editing of materials by Arpena Mesrobian and Lynn Ferrin of the Syracuse University Press.

Finally, I mention the help and cooperation given to me by members of my family. The encouragement and faith shown by my mother and father, most of whose active working years were spent in teaching or in public school and college administration, provided a needed stimulus. Gene, my "long-suffering" wife, and our children, Bob Jr., Scotty, and Mary Ann, have made many personal sacrifices to bring this work to fruition. *The Policy Machine* could not have been written without their understanding of, patience with, and adjustment to my preoccupation with the Department of State.

After recognizing the assistance received from so many sources, I still must accept full responsibility for whatever shortcomings remain in the final product.

Robert E. Elder
Washington, D.C.
March 19, 1960

Contents

Charts

Part One

THE CHALLENGE

1 American Democracy in a Dynamic World
The Search for Survival

THE CHALLENGE

The policy machine which grinds out American foreign policy is one of the most intricate and complex mechanisms of modern democratic government. The totality of operational detail required for its successful functioning is a challenge to individual comprehension. Each policy fired into the murky atmosphere of international relations by the machine must be related to thousands of earlier policies already in orbit, both of our own and foreign design, many of which have been deflected by variables and factors unforeseen at the time of their launching. Although few significant descriptions of the machine have been attempted, a working knowledge of its processes is essential for any practical approach to the substantive issues of foreign policy.

In a sense, the policy machine is nothing more than man writ large, with both his limitations and his potentialities, carrying within itself the frustrations, the interests, and the emotions of contemporary society. For man and the men who make policies are not machines, nor would we have them become mere automatons. Indeed, the ultimate goal of American foreign policy is to preserve and develop the opportunities of mankind to remain human, yet to encourage man to find in himself new humanity. To achieve this end, we plot a course toward tolerance of differing cultures and ideas, assist in the economic and political development of untold millions whose potentialities remain virtually untapped, work for a brave new world in which man can live in peace and friendship with his neighbor. We seek to accomplish the goal without compromising democratic ideals or imposing our

3

way of life on other peoples for whom our form of government or economy is not now and may never be the right one.

We have noble purposes and high aspirations, although we are not always given credit for them abroad and our implementing policies sometimes seem to belie our stated intentions. But much of our national energy in the post-World War II era has been devoted to the negative task of containing an antagonist with whom our relations show little improvement. In spite of American commitments to world affairs unthought of a generation ago, we remain on the treadmill of crisis diplomacy. After almost fifteen years of building, refining, and developing our complicated policy machine into its present form, international tensions are still at dangerous heights. Temporary thaws have been of the January variety, followed by temperatures well below freezing.

Although our tradition is one of resolving differences by discussion, we find ourselves unwilling on occasion to meet with others to negotiate, whatever their purposes, because we claim to be afraid of losing our shirts at the conference table. We alternately pat ourselves on the back for scientific or industrial accomplishment and, looking over our shoulder, view with alarm rapid strides in science and technology elsewhere in the world which appear to threaten our national security. In spite of our own Revolutionary War, we are confounded by militant outbursts of nationalism in colonial and less developed areas. Congressional committees even find it necessary to investigate why it is not safe for a Vice President to visit our allies in Latin America. As American Secretaries of State display remarkably faint enthusiasm for possible hilltop or summit conferences, our friends sometimes seem to be disengaging themselves from us before we can achieve useful disengagement of East and West. This type of analysis may be a caricature of past events, but it serves to make a point. In response to rather alarming developments, we continue to spend billions for survival and, some would say, barely keep our heads above water.

Why is it that we apparently are making such slow progress toward the goal of a better world? Is it sufficient for us to blame those forces at work in the world which compete with us for the minds of men and the resources of the universe? Can we fairly attribute to the Soviet Union the dilemmas of our time and any failures in our foreign policy? What good accrues to America, aside from moral vanity, if we prove our point but are powerless to effect a change?

We are discovering that responsible leadership is a difficult and somewhat thankless task, even at a time when America possesses a relatively favorable power position in the world. What problems will confront us as the populations of other continents and nations are multiplied far beyond our own, if the productive capacities of these areas equal or finally outstrip our industry, if the presently inhibited intellectual capabilities of the less developed peoples should reach full flower, or when another twenty newly independent nations become members of the United Nations?

Whether we like it or not, we can already project developing conditions in foreign areas to a time when our power position is almost certain to be much less favorable than it is today, both within and outside the U.N., when additional states will be strong enough to demand active participation in shaping world affairs. If during our years of leadership and responsibility we waste our sum and substance by exploiting too high a percentage of our resources and manpower primarily for narrow or short-range purposes, searching fruitlessly for absolute security, we may lose our pre-eminent role before a world is created in which all nations can live in relative peace and prosperity. If we fail to exert our democratic strength to help bring such a world into being, or wring our hands helplessly and question the possibility of building a more peaceful world, at some future time nations antagonistic to our way of life, but with a will to sacrifice and more confident in the achievement of their goals, are quite likely to be in the majority among the great powers. Their total resources may counterbalance or even outweigh our own. They may be capable of forcing upon us a secondary role similar to that which they now endure. Under such conditions, what indignities might be heaped upon a once proud nation? Could we expect the treatment of equals from those whom destiny seemed to have thrust up as masters of the world? To defend ourselves, would we sacrifice democracy, become a garrison state?

Although many among us ignore the fact, we are engaged in a race against time, in a search for survival, with no guarantee of success. Can our nation, and the civilization of which it is a part, be boldly imaginative and supremely adaptive, and can it emerge from the evolutionary changes through which society must pass in the last forty years of the twentieth century as a respected and influential partner among nations? History's answer to this question will depend in no small measure upon the organization and effectiveness of the policy machine.

SEARCH FOR SURVIVAL

The Department of State plays a key role in the making of foreign policy. Its mechanisms and personnel, and their relationships to the broader government-wide machinery, have a great influence upon the kind of policy which America will adopt to meet the challenge of our dynamic and confused contemporary world. In a sense, the men and women within the Department of State, who give their thoughts and lives to making the policy machine operate, are conducting a continuous search for the survival of an evolving and ever-changing American way of life.

It is easy to toss verbal brickbats at personalities in the news, especially Secretaries of State; this is one of the freedoms and privileges we enjoy. But the machinery of policy-making has become so massive that the flaws we pick in the performance of personalities may stem from, or be exaggerated by, shortcomings in the machine itself. True, personalities may have predilections which seem to run in channels leading them to make what we consider to be unwise policy decisions. A Pulitzer-prize-winning correspondent who has covered the Department of State with distinction for more than a decade believes that John Foster Dulles, as Secretary of State, was more often right than wrong in dealing with specific or limited problems of foreign policy, such as sending American troops to Lebanon or holding his ground against Communist Chinese pressure on Quemoy and Matsu. If the Dulles stewardship of foreign affairs is to be criticized, according to this well-informed source, it must be for its failure to provide alternate assumptions or find new principles to replace the containment policy inherited from the regime of Secretary of State Dean Acheson. This caused policy to be formulated as a counter to Communist action, it is said, reducing American flexibility and leaving the initiative to the Soviet Union. If one accepts this incisive analysis, Dulles, whatever his faults, may have failed to reorient his attitude on containment toward his own preference for liberation or toward disengagement, because the policy machine was not organized to develop and present the type of ideas which could create such a change.

Policy-makers, particularly those in positions of greatest responsibility, have a workload which staggers the imagination. They have too little time for basic thoughts or reconsideration. They move from problem to problem, without looking much beyond the current crisis. Seminal suggestions or challenging ideas geared to future needs may have to originate at special staff levels before perception and new decisions can provide farsighted redirection of policy from the top.

On an average day, the offices of the Secretary of State and Under Secretary receive 110 telephone calls from outside the Department, 340 telephone calls from inside the Department, 60 letters on requests for action, 45 papers for information, 35 papers for decision, and 25 requests for appointments. This does not include other communications demanding attention, stemming from cabinet meeings, National Security Council meetings, Operations Coordinating Board meetings, press conferences, requests for public appearances, foreign travel or participation in international conferences. In view of this daily avalanche of words and paper, the story told of one post-World War II Secretary of State's first morning in the Department is hardly amusing. He walked through the outer office, cheerily greeting members of his staff gathered there, and disappeared into his private sanctuary. Each assistant, wondering what the great man's first request would be, waited with keen anticipation the ring of the buzzer from the Secretary's desk. An hour passed; then another. At last, on a pretext, a staff member knocked on the Secretary's door and entered. There sat the new Secretary in shirtsleeves, working industriously through the "in" box on his desk, conscientiously writing out his decisions and instructions on implementation in longhand. Adequate procedures by a well-oiled Executive Secretariat [1] make workloads recede to tolerable limits, but it cannot manufacture time for either the Secretary or the Under Secretary to sit like Rodin's thinker and ponder almost unanswerable questions.

The Department itself has been under increasingly mounting pressure in post-World War II years as American policy has become more positive, and American commitments to world affairs have developed breadth and permanence. The Department, with about 6,500 employees in Washington and New York, operates 277 posts overseas, staffed by some 6,100 American citizens and approximately 9,400 alien employees. The communication necessary between the posts and headquarters becomes a sizable task, even if one does not think of the hours and men required to draft the telegrams and reports which the communication system must carry. (The communications flow is handled by the Division of Communications Services in the Office of Operations of the Bureau of Administration.)

On an average day, the Department receives from overseas 419 telegrams, 813 despatches and operations memoranda. The Department despatches in return 1,522 communications by telegraph and diplomatic pouch. During the fiscal year of 1958, a quiet one diplomatically, 7,500,000 words a month flowed in and out through

[1] The Executive Secretariat is a small staff group attached to the Office of the Secretary of State. Its primary function is really threefold. First, it serves as a strainer to make certain that only those documents reach the Secretary and Under Secretary of State which they must see, in proper form, with necessary clearances and ready for action. Second, it serves as a goad to the regional and functional bureaus to make certain that documents needed by the Secretary and Under Secretary will be prepared and forwarded to them in time to meet decision deadlines. Third, as a coordinating device, it distributes information daily in special summaries to the Department's 130 top policy-makers.

the Department's telegraph room. About 1,700 messages of 150 words average length were processed each day. (In a recent year of crisis, the figures were 2,200 and 185.) Eighty per cent of these messages were of a classified nature. In today's complex policy operations, over a hundred copies of many incoming telegrams must be made and distributed through secure channels to officials in the Department and other agencies. Telegraphic traffic is only the beginning. A half million pounds of material is carried annually between American overseas posts and the Department by diplomatic couriers in sealed pouches; almost three quarters of a million more pounds, by air pouch; three million, by surface pouch. This is the raw material, the stuff of which policy is made. (Although one-third of the telegraph traffic and two-thirds of the pouch load are initiated or received for action by government agencies other than the Department which also conduct overseas operations, many of the reports from the field which result from this non-Department flow pass across appropriate desks in the Department in the form of information copies.)

The men in the Department, and the way in which they are organized to do their job, have considerable responsibility for how this mass is digested into policy and what comes out at the top. If there are shortcomings in the men or in the policy machine, they will show up in American foreign policy. For example, we currently have a great many methods or devices at our disposal for the implementation of American foreign policy in any given country overseas, and a budget process which makes it virtually impossible to plan an efficient mix of these methods on an individual country basis.[2]

[2] It has been said that there are 86 such methods for implementing foreign policy. If foreign affairs operations may be thought of as comprehending political, military, economic, informational, or intelligence activities, there are a wide assortment of methods or devices possible within each of these five broad categories. For example, economic activities may involve technical assistance of an agricultural, medical, or educational nature; adustment of tariffs; disposal of surplus agricultural products; outright unilateral grants of money or materials; support of the programs of international agencies like the International Monetary Fund and the International Bank for Reconstruction and Development, Export-Import Bank loans; Development Loan Fund long-term aid; etc.

In the following analysis of the functions and operations of men and machinery in the Department of State, we may discover a survival factor which, if incorporated into the policy-making mechanism, not only will enable America to meet the challenge of our time, but also will insure for America and for Western civilization a positive role in world affairs for centuries to come.

THE GOVERNMENT-WIDE SETTING

The emergence of the United States as one of the two super-powers in the post-World War II era resulted in a proliferation of the agencies of government interested in policy-making and its implementation, and forced signficant readjustments upon the foreign policy mechanism. If the Department of State remained the "strong right arm" of the President in the control of American foreign relations, competing departments or agencies demanded increasing attention and proved useful to the Chief Executive in the conduct of those relations.

In pre-war days, American foreign policy had been rather passive in nature, with political and economic reporting bulking large in the duties of American representatives overseas, along with the performance of consular functions. In such times, the Department of State as the political arm of the President directed negotiations with foreign countries, and in the main it was the Department's "Foreign Service of the United States" which represented the government abroad. As the American role overseas swung abruptly from passivity toward a more directly interventionist approach, government leaders discovered that the implementation of foreign policy required four major types of positive action: political, military, economic, and informational.

An increasing realization of the relationship of power—potential and actual, at home and abroad—to diplomacy elevated the prestige of the Department of Defense in foreign affairs councils. Recognition of the value of economic assistance as a tool of diplomacy led to the establishment of the Economic Cooperation Administration in 1948, which by 1955 had evolved through the Mutual Security Administration and the Foreign Operations Administration into the International Cooperation Administration, now in a semiautonomous position within the Department of State. Also accepted as valuable economic vehicles of foreign policy are the Export-Import Bank—which makes hard loans repayable in dollars, usually for purchasing goods from American sources of supply —and the Development Loan Fund—which makes soft loans repayable in the currency of the borrowing country for economic development projects, often in situations with heavy political overtones. Acceptance of the need for an overseas information and propaganda program caused the creation of an International Information Administration within the Department of State which was finally to become the independent United States Information Agency in 1953. The sky-rocketing costs of the military and economic elements of the new look in American policy brought about a greater involvement of the Treasury Department and the Bureau of the Budget in foreign policy matters. In a sense, departments like Agriculture, Commerce, and Labor, with long-time interests in overseas relationships, have declined in relative importance among the agencies to be consulted in foreign affairs, but in reality their activities have expanded rather than contracted.

This brief recitation of some of the government agencies with a finger in the contemporary foreign policy pie is far from complete, but it suggests the scope of the problem faced by the President in coordinating policy and action today. The task of forging consensus on goals, and an effective degree of consistency in implementing policies designed to achieve them, among powerful departments and agencies was and is a formidable challenge to the concept of Presidential leadership of the executive branch and to the primacy of the Department of State in foreign affairs. Unfortunately, it is almost axiomatic that too many cooks in the American foreign affairs kitchen could spoil the foreign policy soup simmering in the international cauldron.

If the problem of coordination has plagued the President and the Secretary of State in Washington, D.C., it has been no less severe in the field. There, the ability of the ambassador—the President's representative—to mesh the activities of the various government agencies whose operations mushroomed in his country was complicated by two factors:

1. the limited experience of the Department's old-type Foreign Service officers in supervising military, economic, and information operations, or relating them to traditional diplomatic activities, and

2. the appearance overseas of new types of specialist personnel serving on a contract basis or in competing "foreign services."

But the basic problem stemmed from the fact that leaders of American military and economic missions in almost any country had more program money and sometimes more personnel at their disposal than the ambassador. As a result, they were in a position to be— and often were—more influential with foreign governments than the ambassador, who was nominally responsible for American foreign relations with the country. In many countries there was too much free-wheeling and too little effective collaboration among American representatives for policy either to be consistent and effective within a country or of a balanced and integrated nature calculated to contribute to the achievement of global policy goals.

Dispersive forces threatened the effectiveness of policy-making and its implementation both at home and abroad. American Presidents of the era established a close relationship with and placed great reliance upon their Secretaries of State to counteract the centrifugal tendencies debilitating the foreign policy mechanism. Harry Truman was assisted in preserving some unity in American policy by the personal stature of Dean Acheson. Dwight D. Eisenhower was able to rely upon the strong personality of John Foster Dulles during most of his Administration. Nonetheless, both men found it necessary to search for new organizational devices to strengthen or even to maintain Presidential control over foreign affairs, not for the purpose of furthering their personal power but in order to make national power more effective and its expression more consistent. The formation of the National Security Council and the Central Intelligence Agency in 1947 and the Operations Coordinating Board in 1954 must be recognized as major steps toward the achievement of a minimum degree of coordination by the Chief Executive over the foreign affairs agencies.

The National Security Council functions under the National Security Act of 1947, as amended. Serving as a coordinating forum, it is the highest committee in the executive branch of the federal government for the resolution of national security and foreign policy questions. Statutory members include the President, Vice President, Secretary of State, Secretary of Defense, and the Director of the Office of (Civil and) Defense Mobilization. Other government leaders, such as the Secretary of the Treasury and the Director of the Bureau of the Budget, have standing invitations to participate in NSC discussions. Still others are invited when agenda items of interest to their agencies are discussed. Often the Director of the United States Information Agency attends NSC sessions. The Chairman of the Joint Chiefs of Staff and the Director of the Central Intelligence Agency are always present in an advisory capacity.

Backstopping the National Security Council and helping to prepare policy papers for its consideration is the NSC Planning Board, composed of agency representatives of the Assistant Secretary level. The Planning Board itself is serviced by a group of relatively high-ranking civil servants of non-political character who meet regularly and do much of the preliminary work for the Planning Board. A Special Assistant to the President for National Security Affairs acts as chairman of the Planning Board, works closely with the small secretariat attached to the National Security Council, and serves as a link between the NSC and the President. The National Security Council itself does not reach policy decisions, but if its policy papers are approved by the President after discussion and revision, the NSC papers become official statements of United States policy.

The Central Intelligence Agency, now recognized as the leader and coordinator of the Washington intelligence community, was created as the hand-maiden of the National Security Council by the 1947 act which established the NSC. Knowledge of the Agency's actual operations is restricted, but the CIA does gather, analyze, and disseminate information relevant to the formulation of national security and foreign policy. The Agency is headed by a Director of Central Intelligence who, along with the Chairman of the Joint Chiefs of Staff, serves as a principal adviser to the NSC. The work of the Central Intelligence Agency is so compartmentalized that most of its own employees are not aware of its overall organization or procedures. The Agency is believed to have about 10,000 employees in Washington.

It is the duty of a staff in the Central Intelligence Agency to prepare the first composite drafts of the "national intelligence estimates," which are relied upon by policy-planners in the National Security Council for factual information concerning the present and the possible future conditions of foreign countries. A national intelligence estimate usually contains a factual description of the present situation and a two- to five-year projection of what conditions are likely to become in an individual country or region. It represents the combined thinking of the various intelligence agencies and provides a basis for the formation of long-term policy recommendations within the NSC structure. The CIA draft of a national intelligence estimate concerning any given country is discussed and approved—or differences of opinion noted—in middle level inter-agency discussions before being forwarded for discussion and final approval by the United States Intelligence Board. The USIB is composed of the directors of intelligence units in the agencies of government carrying on intelligence activities. Approved national estimates are the factual basis for NSC discussion and Presidential decision.

When it became evident that implementation of National Security Council policies approved by the President was uneven in, or subject to a variety of interpretations by, the participating departments and agencies, the Operations Coordinating Board was established in 1954. The OCB consists of officials at the Under Secretary level, and its membership is roughly parallel to that of the NSC. The Operations Coordinating Board's function is to develop in programmatic detail the general policies developed in the NSC structure and approved by the President. It attempts to facilitate voluntary acceptance of specific responsibilities by the several participating departments and agencies. Periodically, it reports to the NSC on the progress being made in the implementation of NSC policies. The OCB has its own secretariat and a Presidential Special Assistant for Security Operations Coordination. It has its own group of Board assistants. Approximately fifty OCB inter-departmental working groups backstop the OCB's policy imple-mentation activities, preparing OCB policy statements and reports on progress in policy implementation for the consideration of the OCB Board assistants. Each interdepartmental working group is responsible for a particular regional area, individual country, or functional problem.

The growth of these three coordinating mechanisms—NSC, CIA and OCB—has contributed in some ways to strengthening Presidential leadership in policy-making and to increasing cooper-ation of agencies under ambassadorial leadership on "country teams" in the field. Nonetheless, the use of the committee system in the preparation of papers for policy-making, implementation, and intelligence has also occasionally allowed the agencies to keep their differences to themselves, to compromise short of the President, so that all alternatives and divergent interests would not be made clearly apparent to him. Also, it must be realized that teamwork in the field is more easily adopted as official policy than actually achieved. Furthermore, while these organizations have formalized processes of coordination, it should be observed that many informal clearances between agencies took place before the National Security Council was set up and still occur on questions which are not taken up within the NSC structure.

Many of the papers which work up through the NSC-CIA-OCB complex are largely based on early drafts written by relatively low-level personnel, such as the country desk officer and area or functional intelligence analysts in the Department of State. Decisions made by Presidents and Secretaries of State are greatly influenced by staffwork performed at the country desk and a variety of intervening levels. Therefore, to develop an under-standing of the Department of State—the policy machine—in its government-wide setting, it appears helpful to start at the bottom of the totem pole in the Department with the country desk officer.

Moving onward from this vantage point, an unhurried look at other major elements in Department policy-making may be rewarding to us collectively if it is sufficiently thought-provoking to each of us individually.

Part Two

POLICY - MAKING

2 Country Desk Officer
Low Man on the Totem Pole

IMPORTANCE OF THE DESK

A country desk officer in one of the regional bureaus of the Department of State may be low man on the totem pole so far as seniority in policy-making is concerned, yet he wields significant power in the formulation of American foreign policy. With a considerable degree of truth, it may be said of him that he is both wheelhorse and sparkplug of the decision-making process.

Policy-making in the Department of State is centered in five regional bureaus, which in turn are composed of sub-regional offices. (See Chart 1 for the basic structure of the Department of State.) The five regional bureaus cover (1) European Affairs, (2) Far Eastern Affairs, (3) Near Eastern and South Asian Affairs, (4) Inter-American Affairs, and (5) African Affairs. (The Bureau of International Organization Affairs is often considered a sixth regional bureau because it is responsible for Department relations with the American mission to the United Nations. It assumes action responsibility for items on the United Nation's agenda, in the same fashion that the five recognized regional bureaus are responsible for relations with their assigned areas.)

The bureaus maintain close contact with American embassies in their respective continental areas of responsibility, receiving despatches from abroad and sending out policy instructions. An Assistant Secretary of State heads each regional bureau. He serves in somewhat the same capacity as an operating vice president in the business world. Below him in the hierarchy are his Office Directors, each responsible for operations in a small group of countries. The country desk officer is at the bottom of this heap. He usually con-

19

CHART 1

SOME BASIC ELEMENTS IN THE STRUCTURE OF THE DEPARTMENT OF STATE

Director, Executive Secretariat

Secretary
Under Secretary

Under Secretary for Political Affairs

Director, International Cooperation Administration

Assistant Secretary, Policy Planning Staff

Assistant Secretary, Bureau of Economic Affairs	Special Assistant to the Secretary, Bureau of International Cultural Relations	The Director, Bureau of Intelligence and Research
Office of International Financial and Development Affairs	Cultural Policy and Development Staff	Office of Current Intelligence Indications
Office of International Trade	International Educational Exchange Service	Office of Research and Analysis for American Republics
Office of International Resources	UNESCO Relations Staff	Office of Research and Analysis for Asia
Office of Transport and Communications	Secretariat of the U.S. Advisory Commission on Educational Exchange and the Advisory Committee on the Arts	Office of Research and Analysis for Mid-East and Africa
Mutual Defense Assistance Control Staff	East-West Contacts Staff	Office of Research and Analysis for Sino-Soviet Bloc
	Cultural Presentations Staff	Office of Research and Analysis for Western Europe
		Office of Functional and Biographic Intelligence
		Functional Intelligence Division
		External Research Division
		Biographic Information Division
		Office of Intelligence Resources and Coordination
		Intelligence Collection and Distribution Division
		The Library Division

Assistant Secretary, Bureau of African Affairs	Assistant Secretary, Bureau of Inter-American Affairs	Assistant Secretary, Bureau of European Affairs

Diplomatic Missions, Consular Offices, and Delegations to International Organizations

Special Assistants		

		Director General, Foreign Service
Deputy Under Secretary for Political Affairs	Deputy Under Secretary for Administration	Foreign Service Institute
Assistant Secretary, Congressional Relations	Legal Adviser	Foreign Service Inspection Corps

Assistant Secretary, Bureau of Public Affairs	Assistant Secretary, Bureau of Administration	Administrator, Bureau of Security and Consular Affairs
Policy Plans and Guidance Staff Office of News Office of Public Services Historical Office Public Opinion Studies Staff Mutual Security Information Staff	Office of Budget Office of Finance Office of Personnel Office of Operations Foreign Reporting Staff Cryptography Staff Office of Foreign Buildings Regulations and Procedures Staff	Passport Office Visa Office Office of Special Consular Services Office of Security Office of Munitions Control Office of Refugee and Migration Affairs

Assistant Secretary, Bureau of Far Eastern Affairs	Assistant Secretary, Bureau of Near Eastern and South Asian Affairs	Assistant Secretary, Bureau of International Organization Affairs

cerns himself, subject to supervision and review from above, with policy toward a single foreign nation.

In the comfortable, pre-World War II days, when the Department still had less than 1,000 employees, policy-making was the responsibility of small regional divisions which dealt through desk officers with American embassies and legations overseas. Desk officers were in close contact with the single Assistant Secretary of State who headed the regional divisions, and often consulted directly with the Secretary of State. The growing workload of the Department during and after World War II, with a concurrent increase in personnel and almost continuous reorganization, changed the divisions to offices and then to bureaus. The country desk officer worked at the same old last, but the hierarchy above him became more complex. The Office Director separated him from regular contact with his Assistant Secretary, now one among five Assistant Secretaries heading regional bureaus. An Under Secretary for Political Affairs lessened the need for consultation with the Secretary of State, who had become much too busy to see desk officers anyway.

In spite of these changes, the Department's 114 country desk officers remain the eyes and ears, the brain and voice, of America in a troubled world. They keep daily watch over events in 179 political entities from Aden through Zanzibar. Almost every scrap of information which government agencies collect on an area and many policy papers from other agencies proposing action in an area cross the country desk, at a rate of 250 to 350 documents per day. (The desk man learns to get the gist of a document in ten seconds, to know whether he must read it in detail or not.) The desk remains the real contact point in the Department for the diplomatic post abroad and the foreign embassy in Washington.

As the drafting officer who usually is first to put policy ideas on paper, the desk man is in a sense the initiator of American policy toward his assigned country. He writes telegrams, memoranda, and even more formal policy papers. His drafts, perhaps modified by a superior but many times not touched at all, often reach an Assistant Secretary of State, may go in revised form before the

National Security Council for consideration and final decision by the President. In whatever form his broad policy paper may at last be adopted by the NSC, he is likely to be consulted in the drafting of the Operations Coordinating Board's more specific paper on how the NSC policy shall be implemented. Later, he will draft OCB progress reports on actual implementation, how policy operations are progressing in the field, subject to the opinion and attitudes of others in an OCB working group.

The desk man's influence at all levels in the decision-making process stems from his detailed knowledge of an area and his role as a drafting officer. Unless he is really out of step, it is easier for his bosses to concur or make minor revisions than to disagree and upset his apple cart. The "tyranny of the written word" works in his favor. On day-to-day routine matters, the desk officer is cock of the walk. He may have considerable influence upon policy decisions at higher levels. However, his room for maneuver in the formulation of policy is not too great. He is quite conscious of the views of his superiors. He does not make policy in a vacuum.

The basic assumptions and broad goals of American policy already considered by the National Security Council and approved by the President, as well as implementing policies previously formulated by the Operations Coordinating Board, quickly become an inherent part of his thinking. These are likely to be of a relatively stable and continuing nature, pre-dating his coming to the desk. They tend to set the limits within which he will operate on policy matters, for agonizing reappraisals are more likely to come from above than from below. The desk man has an opportunity to know public, legislative, and executive opinion in America and abroad. This knowledge limits the practical alternatives open to his consideration. His recommendations on unusual or controversial questions are thoroughly reviewed. After all, he is low man on the foreign policy-making totem pole. There is no question of the right of those above him to disapprove policies he proposes or to force revision of his proposals. This authority is often used. Members of the Department of State Policy Planning Staff, as well as regional and functional planners, have as one of their major

functions the development of policy statements which may be
approved by top Department officials. True, the desk officer is
likely to be consulted as work progresses if the policy involves his
country directly, but broader regional and functional considerations may minimize the effectiveness of his argument. The desk
officer must fall in line.

When the chips are down and an international crisis flares, the
desk officer may take part with his Office Director and Assistant
Secretary in "telecon" conferences with posts overseas. He may
work round the clock drafting instructions to the American embassy in his country. But these are subject to review by the Assistant Secretary. If it is a question of peace or war, the decision
is made at an even higher level. At such a time, the Secretary,
Under Secretary, and Under Secretary for Political Affairs may
consider the Department's recommendations with the Deputy
Under Secretary for Administration and the Assistant Secretaries.
The final executive decision may be taken by the President, probably after informal consultation with several trusted members of
the National Security Council. The narrower country interests
of the desk officer are buried under this parade of high brass. It
is just as well. There is no time for paperwork. The discussions are
face to face. The decisions must be immediate, the considerations
global.

THE FOREIGN SERVICE TYPE

There is probably no such thing as a typical desk officer, but
there have been those who once served at the desk level who could
be defined as the "desk officer type," in the same way that William
S. White defines the "senate type" in *Citadel*, "a man for whom
the Institution is a career in itself, a life in itself and an end in
itself." [1] In the good old days (at least a decade ago), before
Wristonization [2] with its integration of Department personnel into

---

[1] William Smith White, *Citadel*, New York: Harper and Brothers, 1957.

[2] The term "Wristonization" is derived from the fact that Henry M. Wriston,
while still President of Brown University, served as chairman of the committee
which recommended the integration of Departmental and Foreign Service personnel. The purpose was to better acquaint Foreign Service officers with the

the Foreign Service, during the mid-1950's, the desk officer type—though certainly always in a minority among the Department's desk officers—must have existed and even flourished. Indeed, he was often viewed with alarm by young Foreign Service officers in the field. They knew him neither by sight nor sound but doubted that he understood their areas, their recommendations, or the necessity of ever taking prompt action. They did know he had a veritable worship of forms and red tape and found reporting officers at posts abroad wretched creatures of incomparable imperfection.

The situation of endless tenure on the desk, coupled with a condition of permanent servitude in the field, which led to so many misunderstandings in the past, no longer abounds. By and large, the desk officer type either has gone to his reward, been retired, transferred to another agency, or—worst of all—been sent to the field. His replacement is usually a "Foreign Service type," younger, more flexible, easier to get along with, certainly much better fitted in many ways for the rough-and-tumble exigencies of policy-making in the hydrogen missile and earth satellite age. This new type comes from the field, often with several years of specialized training and experience before assignment, works the desk for no more than four years, and returns to the field.

One speaks of the "Foreign Service type" without derogation; the appellation can be viewed only as a symbol of forthright flattery by anyone who knows the modern country desk officer. College-trained and usually in his late thirties or early forties, the Foreign Service type desk officer is personable and intelligent, possessing some verbal skill, considerable initiative, and a sense

---

problems at home, and the Department staff members with the situation in the field. "Wristonees" are the Department officers, formerly in the Civil Service and subject only to assignment in Washington, who were accepted into the Foreign Service and became subject to assignment overseas. As a result of the implementation of the Wriston Committee's recommendations, additional positions were opened to Foreign Service officers in the Department—including many at the desk officer level. Conversely, many "Wristonees"—including a number of former desk officers—were sent abroad for service at American embassies or legations. If this new flexibility of assignment solved some problems, it created others. For a further discussion of Wristonization, see Chapter 9.

of responsibility. It is expected of this modern Foreign Service type desk officer that he be as American as Hoosier fried chicken, as moral as the man who sits next to you in church on Sunday, and as mature and agile of mind as a senior member of a university faculty. He must possess a cosmopolitan urbanity which provides him with an ability to be at home with people, either at a hot dog roast in suburbia or a caviar and cocktail affair on embassy row. The latter he counts as business rather than pleasure. Not all desk officers measure up equally well to every one of these demanding specifications, but the Foreign Service type—with his enthusiasm, tolerance, and sense of humor—will have a good try at meeting these requirements. Failure to achieve perfection does not particularly bother him. The Foreign Service type, in contrast with the desk officer type, readily confesses that he is occasionally fallible, that to err is human. This modest admission is one of his most engaging traits.

Since Wristonization, the dream of every real Foreign Service type is to hold down a country desk in the Department of State at one point in his career; the enchanting vision is before him always, once he passes his written and oral examinations and is inducted into the Foreign Service of the United States. Such a coveted assignment will be ample compensation for years at lonely outposts overseas. Not that he necessarily wants a Washington tour. Living conditions are expensive, adequate housing difficult to find, servants out of the question; all this is quite upsetting to Foreign Service wives, if an Americanizing influence upon their children. But if the Foreign Service type goes to Washington at all, he hopes it will be to the desk. He views the desk not only as an end in itself but as a steppingstone toward further preferment in the Foreign Service.

Policy-making and political operations are the primary functions for which the Department of State is in business, but the successful carrying on of line tasks requires adequate supplemental staffing. In the interest of building a well-balanced Foreign Service, many young officers are assigned Departmental tours of duty in the fields of intelligence, administration, and public affairs

—possibly as economic or political analysts in functional bureaus. The true Foreign Service type serves faithfully but rather unhappily when assigned Department duty outside the regional bureaus. Almost always, he continues to cast a wistful eye toward the desk. There the responsibility appears to be more directly related to policy formulation and operations. These are the functions he considers to be the essence of his life's work.

Even if the desk has lost some of its direct personal relationship with the Secretary of State, as the Department has grown in response to American assumption of leadership in an increasingly complex world, the desk has lost little of its attraction or glamour. It is true that the desk officer no longer serves as a "little despot," making policy on the cables. More and more consideration must be given to the wishes of other areas and bureaus within the Department, to the conflicting interests of other departments, and to the coordinating agencies like the National Security Council and the Operations Coordinating Board. American policy-makers face the necessity of developing some consistency between policies toward individual states, for entire regions, and of a global nature. Today, country policy is a small cog which must mesh in several larger wheels. Even so, with the increasing stature of the United States in world politics and the positive rather than the passive role now played by America overseas, the Foreign Service type may have a greater net influence upon international affairs than did his desk officer type predecessor (in spite of a loss of power in relationship to other groups in the Department or outside it).

Let us make a necessary but small point. The Department of State distinguishes between the terms "desk officer" and "officer in charge." There is, for example, an Officer in Charge of France-Iberia Affairs. There is also a French desk officer. There is presumably a single desk officer for Spain and Portugal. The desk officers, in this case, are guided to some extent in their operations by their officer in charge. In most bureaus, an officer in charge can initiate and send a telegram of routine instructions to the field over the Secretary of State's signature without clearing with a superior officer. A desk officer may draft such a telegram, but the authority for sending it would rest with the officer in charge.

For present purposes, both officers in charge and desk officers fall loosely under our working phrase, desk officer. "Officer in charge" sounds more pretentious and may be best suited to the desk officer type of recent memory, but the modest title of "desk officer" well befits all the hard-working, quick-witted young men who today fill these closely related posts.

Enough has been said of the function and nature of the desk officer in the regional bureaus of the Department of State to indicate the degree of his importance to an understanding of the foreign policy decision-making process. A more detailed look at how he performs his duties is desirable.

SOURCES OF INFORMATION

Without a constant flow of information, the Department of State might just as well shut up shop. Furthermore, the right facts must reach the right people at the right time. In most instances, sufficient facts—and a great many more—are available at the proper time for the performance of the desk officer's policy-making operations. The success of the efficient flow of information and policy papers through the Department must be attributed in some measure to the Executive Secretariat, which monitors the process from on high, as an adjunct to the Office of the Secretary.

The desk man's most important source of information is the American Foreign Service post abroad. Embassies send daily telegrams on questions requiring immediate action. Despatches via diplomatic courier or air mail pouch include additional detail. Each week the post forwards a broad report covering political, economic, and military developments, the so-called "weeka." It includes information on cultural, psychological, agricultural, and other aspects of national life. Conditions are viewed with more perspective in quarterly, semi-annual, and annual reports from the post. At some posts, in addition, eager beaver Foreign Service type officers prepare a thorough round-up despatch a year after being assigned to a country, and another when they finish their tour of duty. This is a valuable training device and also yields useful information for the desk officer in the Department.

Daily political, economic, and military intelligence reports are available to desk officers. These are of value in day-to-day operations. By the time the Central Intelligence Agency's weekly summary reaches the desk, its information may be old stuff, but its evaluative comment is appreciated. Information copies of detailed reports by our embassy attachés to the departments of Defense, Commerce, Treasury, Agriculture, Labor, the International Cooperation Administration, and the United States Information Agency also pass across the desk. They are useful as background but not for daily operations.

News stories and editorial comment from leading foreign newspapers are wired daily from some embassies to the desk. Press clippings air mailed from the post are a more common practice. Foreign language newspapers and periodicals published in the United States are also received. Desk officers interested in our good neighbors to the South read *Diario Las Americas* and the Latin American edition of *Time*. Press reports are not official, but Department news tickers sometimes carry information before it comes from the post. Associated Press, United Press International, and Reuters ticker reports from the Office of News are fanned out to the desks every hour. Press clippings from twenty-eight American papers are distributed daily.

Summaries of editorial comment in the American press are circulated each day to many desks by the Department's Public Opinion Studies Staff. A monthly summary sets public opinion in a broader context. Special studies give more detailed analyses of American attitudes toward policy in specific areas. The desk officer is less interested in this material than higher-ranking officers in the Department who must wrestle more directly with the question of political feasibility.

The *New York Times* is the desk officer's favorite newspaper. At the office, in most bureaus, he reads a marked copy which indicates articles or comments related to his country. More leisurely reading at home may fill him in on other world developments.

Contact with scholarly publications may be maintained by regular routing of periodicals from the Library Division or by personal subscription. One desk man in the Bureau of Far Eastern Affairs, for example, reads the *Far Eastern Quarterly, Foreign Affairs,* and the *Annals of the American Academy of Political and Social Sciences.* Interest of desk officers in this type of publication is quite uneven.

The desk officer does little of his own research. Some pertinent research information appears in studies prepared for the Senate Foreign Relations and House Foreign Affairs Committees by the Legislative Reference Service or on contract by outside consultants. Within the Department, the desk obtains specialized research studies from the Bureau of Intelligence and Research, the Historical Office, the Legal Adviser, and the Bureau of Economic Affairs.

Embassies of foreign nations in Washington often have less basic data available on their countries than the desk officer. Informal and formal relations between the desk and embassy are primarily of use in providing operational information.

THE DAILY ROUTINE

Since no desk officer can ever count ahead of time upon a routine day, a single day's schedule of one desk officer's activities may not be typical of all desk men's routines, but it is revealing:

8:45–9:15 A.M.   Reads incoming correspondence and telegrams from the field. (Actually, he often arrives at 8:00 A.M. to do this.) Takes action as necessary. Reads newspaper.

9:15–10:00 A.M.   Daily staff conference with other desk officers, chaired by his Office Director. (The Office Director has just come from the Assistant Secretary's staff conference.)

10:00–11:45 A.M.   Conference with representatives from State, Agriculture, and the International Cooperation Administration to agree on text of a grant to his country under Public Law 480 dealing with the disposal of surplus agricultural commodities.

11:45–12:45 P.M.   Drafts telegram to American embassy overseas, informing it of present stage of developments on grant. Carries telegram by hand around Department for clearance.

12:45–1:45 P.M. Drafts tentative copy of formal *Department Instructions* which will go to American embassy overseas to accompany text of proposed grant.

1:45–2:15 P.M. Lunch.

2:15–3:00 P.M. Writes a personal and informal letter to the Chargé d'Affaires in the American embassy overseas to explain the proposed grant.

3:00–4:00 P.M. Attends special conference to brief the Under Secretary of Commerce who is going to a trade fair in his country as the President's representative. The desk officer details political and economic conditions in the country and explains cultural differences.

4:00–4:30 P.M. Briefs a teacher who is going to his country on an exchange program. Discusses housing problems, the country's educational system, research facilities, as well as political, economic and social conditions.

4:30–5:30 P.M. Reads memoranda and telegrams which have come to his desk during day for clearance. Writes comments or recommendations.

5:30–6:00 P.M. (He's working overtime again.) Reads reports from field and other sources of information which have come to his desk during the day.

In addition to these formally recorded events, there were a number of phone calls, both in and out—for example, one from a member of Congress, another from a businessman with interests in the desk man's country, one to the country's embassy in Washington, another from it. Also, he checked several matters with desk officers in neighboring offices and, on one occasion, sought the advice of his Office Director. There happened to be no face-to-face relations with any representative of his country's embassy during this particular day.

Relations of the desk and embassy may be either business or social, official functions or informal gatherings. Minor business is discussed by telephone or by a visit of someone from the embassy to the desk. The range of problems arising in embassy-desk relations is great and may include matters of either private or public concern. The parents of a child stricken by polio in a foreign land appeal through their embassy in Washington for special treatment available only in the United States. The embassy arranges for free care by a private agency. When the mother arrives in America with her child, there is a misunderstanding about arrangements with the agency. To whom does the embassy turn for advice and assistance? Several phone calls by the desk officer resolve the difficulty. A husband whose nationality is that of the desk officer's country unthoughtfully murders his wife, a former United States citizen. Her brother is an American citizen. The husband is put in jail. The brother gains custody of the children and brings them to the United States. The husband's wealthy family in the desk officer's country seeks through the embassy in Washington to gain custody of the children. Who is right in the middle of the tugging and hauling? The desk officer, of course.

The ambassador may call at the Department in person if his government's interests are directly involved. When he talks with an appropriate Assistant Secretary or the Under Secretary, the desk officer is usually present. The ambassador may present a "note" or leave an *aide memoire*. If the ambassador informs the Department ahead of time as to the subject of his visit, the desk officer draws up a "briefing memorandum" for the Assistant Secretary, including background information and a recommended American position. If the subject is not known, the memorandum covers several possible topics. Immediately after the meeting, the desk officer prepares a "memorandum of conversation" for the Assistant Secretary. He also writes the first draft of any reply necessitated by the discussion. Information copies of both go in final form to interested posts overseas and government agencies in Washington.

An agreement may have been reached between the foreign embassy and the Department for the transfer of surplus equipment at an airfield abroad. The desk officer drafts a third person note to the foreign embassy expressing the Department's pleasure at agreement. "The Department will arrange for the details of transfer." He sends a telegram advising the American post overseas of the agreement. If he has intimate knowledge which will be useful to the post in making the transfer, he writes a personal letter to some member of the staff. He also draws up detailed formal instructions to the American embassy, outlining the transfer process: documents involved, who must sign, number and routing of copies.

From time to time the desk officer is drawn into the process of drafting position papers to guide American negotiators at the United Nations or attending special international conferences. Papers of this type require coordination with other regional or functional bureaus and cooperation with the Bureau of International Organization Affairs. The position paper (with background, discussion, and recommendations) can be a challenging task to the desk officer. He must set in historical context the position which states have previously taken on the problem, anticipate the maximum and minimum demands of those likely to oppose the American position, suggest maximum and minimum positions for the United States. Then he must discuss this variety of possible positions, presenting the arguments for each. Finally, he sums up and justifies a set of policy recommendations.

No less a challenge is the desk officer's role in congressional relations. If legislation which is to be proposed to Congress by the Department may affect his country, an officer is drawn into discussions within the Department during the legislative drafting sessions. He may participate later in conferences with other agencies and with representatives of the Bureau of the Budget in getting clearance for such legislative measures within the executive branch. When the bill has been introduced and reaches a congressional committee for hearings, the desk man is likely to testify before an executive session of the committee.

He is also drawn into the answering of Department mail from a congressional source. Such letters are routed into the Department by the Bureau of Congressional Relations and must be answered within three days. If an official policy statement cannot be cleared within that time, the desk officer must notify the Congressman by phone or letter why an answer is not immediately forthcoming, and approximately when an answer can be given. Even questions posed to the Department by a Congressman on behalf of his constituents are sometimes forwarded to the desk officer for a reply.

Not all of the desk officer's daily routine is paperwork. He has many visitors, most not connected with embassies. They must be interspersed with drafting, clearances, conferences, staff meetings, and telephone calls. He talks with researchers or social workers going out to his area, to business men with interests abroad, and to ordinary citizens with family problems in a foreign country. The telephone is indispensable to the desk officer. As the center of information in the Department on a certain country, all sorts of queries are directed to him. If he doesn't know the answer, he has to know where to get it. He has information contacts throughout the Department and in many other government agencies. Without the telephone, the desk officer could not gather spot information from his colleagues nor get rapid and informal clearance of notes to embassies, telegrams and instructions to the field, or policy papers (not to mention letters to Congressmen).

CLEARANCE AND COORDINATION

Many desk officers prefer to keep paperwork at a minimum and consult or exchange information in person with fellow desk officers or their immediate superior, the Office Director. Others are confirmed "paper pushers," memorandum writers who send most information up the line or to other desks in typed form. Information in a despatch reaching the desk from the field may be important enough to demand consideration at higher levels. The desk officer summarizes the despatch, makes a recommendation, and forwards the memorandum to his Office Director. The despatch, with important sections underlined, goes along as an attachment.

Normally, a memorandum is drafted on any question to be considered by an Assistant Secretary. Memoranda are factual, usually a page in length, and hardly ever more than three. Over a third conclude with a policy recommendation. New desk officers send more problems to the office of their Assistant Secretary for review than do experienced desk men. If the question is controversial, like East-West relations or Tunisian-French relations, the desk seeks guidance. The Office Director forwards memoranda on matters of sufficient importance—approved or disapproved—to the Assistant Secretary.

Failure by the desk officer to obtain clearance from other bureaus in the Department or from other government agencies with a direct interest in a note, telegram, or policy paper means that agreement must be sought at a higher level or the matter dropped. An attempt is made to solve a problem at as low a level as possible. The purpose is not to arrogate power but to reduce the burden on the Assistant Secretary and those above him. The policy-making pyramid narrows rapidly, with fewer decision-makers and broader areas of authority at the top. Department leaders must be protected from being literally smothered in their offices by the flow of paper. Even with efficient screening of materials which reach them, these men work under constant pressure.

A single problem concerning Near Eastern oil may involve the country desk officer for Iran and desk officers for the USSR, Great Britain, the United Arab Republic, Jordan, and Saudi Arabia; representatives of the Bureaus of Intelligence and Research, Economic Affairs, International Organization Affairs, and Congressional Relations; plus desk officers or specialists from the Central Intelligence Agency, the Departments of Defense and Commerce, the International Cooperation Administration, and the United States Information Agency.

When a policy statement prepared by the desk officer for Iran runs into trouble in the clearance process—and how can it avoid being tempest-tossed with such a variety of interests to be accommodated—a conference of interested bureaus and agencies is held at the desk level to attempt a resolution of differences. If this fails, the question may go up to the Office Director, with a recommendation from the desk. The Office Director checks with others at his level in the Department and other agencies. If speed is of the essence and problems continue to separate the interested parties, the question must be forwarded to the Assistant Secretary and arrangements made for an inter-agency conference at this relatively high level. If this meeting does not produce agreement, the Under Secretary for Political Affairs or perhaps his deputy will take a crack at resolving differences with his peers in other departments and agencies. (By this time, at least, the Department itself must be pretty much united on the issue.) The search for a solution may require direct intervention by the Under Secretary or the Secretary of State himself. When the question is of such national importance that differences must be resolved and action taken, disagreement among departments at the Under Secretary or Secretary level sends the problem to the National Security Council, after as thorough staff preparation as time will allow, for a final decision by the President. As the sign said on President Harry Truman's desk when he was in the White House, "The buck stops here."

At any point along this passing of the problem to higher ranking officials, if the splits between the departments and agencies are obviously so great that further discussion at intermediate levels is useless, the question can be transferred to the National Security Council machinery. The desk officer is not free of the problem when the question starts its upward trek. But, the higher the matter goes, the less influence the desk officer is likely to exert upon the final decision. He is consulted at all levels and may draft several revisions of the original memorandum. The rather simple early draft may eventually be rewritten by the desk officer as a formal problem paper, complete with background, statement of problem, possible alternatives with pros and cons of each, and a brief recommendation.

Once it is apparent that the National Security Council machinery will come into play, the question may be reviewed and some revision of the paper made by the Department of State's Policy Planning Staff which backstops the Secretary, preparing him for National Security Council discussions. The desk officer is likely to be consulted by the Policy Planning Staff if it considers the problem. The paper passes through the Planning Board Assistants and reaches the Planning Board of the National Security Council for final overhaul before at last attaining the ultimate level of consideration, the National Security Council. The desk officer could conceivably appear before all three groups. (On the other hand, such a *tour de force* is highly unlikely, and he has usually been forgotten long since.)

After a decision is made by the President, with the assistance of the National Security Council, the policy paper goes to the Operations Coordinating Board for implementation. National Security Council papers are usually rather general, spelling out purposes and goals rather than precisely how these may be achieved. So, the Operations Coordinating Board decides how to implement in more specific detail the somewhat broader outline laid down by the NSC. The OCB, working through its Board Assistants, reaches down to the desk officer for drafts to be considered by OCB working groups on implementation of NSC policies. Progress reports on approved policies implementing NSC decisions must be submitted annually by the OCB to the NSC, assessing what has been accomplished, what new problems loom on the horizon. The desk officer, of course, is a member of the OCB inter-agency working group which prepares the progress report and may actually be the group's drafting officer and acting chairman. The Office Director may be the formal chairman. It may take a series of conferences over a period of two or three months to achieve agreement on a three- to five-page progress report.

Now while the desk officer is busy following the problem related to his country up and down the policy ladder, countless (113 anyway) other desk officers are busily engaged at different stages of the same process, focusing upon a wide variety of problems in other countries. In such a helter-skelter disarrangement, the problem of coordination of information and knowledge of actions taken becomes vital. There is no set pattern of coordination of information imposed from above on the bureaus of the Department. As a result, the variety of coordinating devices is impressive, but no one bureau employs all of them. This may be just as well or all the desk officer's time would be taken up with coordination. He would have no time left to accomplish his regularly assigned tasks.

In at least one regional bureau of the Department, each desk officer keeps a country briefing book up to date. This includes general background data, the political and economic situation, United States agency projects in the country, and a discussion of relations with the United States. The briefing book is useful to the President, Vice President, or members of Congress when they travel abroad, to other government leaders from the executive branch attending international conferences or trade fairs in foreign countries, and for ready reference at the desk or other levels within the Department. In another bureau, the desk officers maintain a country policy book. This is a careful statement of American policy toward the country. It indicates pressing problems and is revised every three months. The briefing or policy books from within these bureaus reach the Assistant Secretary. Each is reproduced and collated for distribution within the bureaus to Office Directors and desk officers. Such books may help to achieve coordination of information and policy. There is no unanimous acceptance of the internal value of such briefing books, however. Since it is the men at the desk level who must keep them up to date, it is little wonder that some of them feel that the books are more trouble than they are worth.

Fortunately, some degree of coordination is attained by briefing and policy books, the necessity of clearance, and conferences on policy papers. In addition, staff meetings held daily in some bureaus, or two or three times per week in others, spread information and policy guidance from the Secretary through intervening levels to the desk officer and vice versa on a regular basis. The Secretary meets with his advisers of Assistant Secretary rank and above every morning at 9:15. After an intelligence briefing, views are exchanged on important problems raised by the Secretary or by other participants. Assistant Secretaries hold regular meetings with their Office Directors; Office Directors, with desk officers. Each of the meetings provides an opportunity for information or

instructions to be passed down, and for information, recommendations, or requests for guidance to be passed up. Ideas from the
Secretary coming down often meet with ideas coming up from
the desk officers at the Assistant Secretary level. Concentration in
this analysis upon the role of the desk officer does not alter the fact
that the focal point of decision-making on most important problems confronting the Department is the office of an Assistant Secretary.

Although personal contact between the desk officer and the
Secretary has seriously diminished, for obvious reasons, it is an
untruth to say that no policy guidance is given by Department
leaders to desk officers. Equally untrue is the myth that leaders are
unaware of what desk officers are thinking (even though their
thoughts may occasionally be ignored). In all fairness, something
of what a desk officer is trying to communicate orally at a staff
meeting may be lost in the distillation process going through the
Office Director and the Assistant Secretary to the Secretary. But,
something also may be gained. "Big democracy" poses problems of
organization and coordination.

Secretary of State John Foster Dulles held press conferences
almost every Tuesday he was in Washington. Christian Herter has
held such conferences much less regularly.

Answers to the questions anticipated at a Dulles conference
were drafted by desk officers on Monday afternoon, cleared by
Office Directors and Assistant Secretaries, and placed in the Secretary's hands by Monday evening or Tuesday morning. By Tuesday afternoon, the desk officer could read the Department's press
release on the conference (or any Washington newspaper) and
know what use or adaptation the Secretary had made of his views.

Possibly emphasis on policy guidance as here described, both
up and down, seems to be on a day-to-day treadmill. This does not
mean that longer-range policy (looking two, five, or ten years
ahead) is completely ignored or does not receive some attention.
It does indicate that there must be a constant effort to escape the
worm's eye view in order to attain sufficient perspective for foresighted decision-making. Basic policy decisions are now made

at the National Security Council level by the President. These
serve as rather broad guide lines to the Department of State. Department officials, including the desk officers, play an integral part
in the formation of National Security Council policy and in its
implementation by the Operations Coordinating Board. They are
conscious of it as they make day-to-day decisions. On rare occasions, a desk officer will prepare a basic problem paper on his own
initiative and forward it up the line on a question of somewhat
longer-range policy. The primary responsibility assigned the Department's Policy Planning Staff is to assist in the formulation of
such policy. As we have seen, the Planning Staff usually consults
with desk officers or their immediate superiors at some stage in
its deliberations.

One major shortcoming of policy problem papers and policy
statements is that changing conditions put each crisis into a slightly
different context from that in which it was originally conceived.
This requires revision of policy papers, such as those formulated
by the NSC and OCB, and new crash decisions to meet the realities
of a developing situation. The thinking which has already been
done about the problem is far from lost; it may be put to good
use. Under conditions of crisis, timing and blending of American
policies with those of other countries become of utmost importance. The more you know and have agreed to ahead of time, the
faster you can consider new facts and act. The overwhelming
necessities of the moment may require decisions which appear to
be inconsistent with previously formulated NSC-OCB policy. If
there has been sufficient earlier consideration of awkward con-
tingencies in relevant NSC papers, one step backward may be a
firm platform from which two steps forward may be taken when
the crisis abates.

The organization of the Department of State, with the desk
officer at its heart, is complex but relatively efficient. The decision
process, as pointed out, is flexible and can be speeded in time of
emergency. It is fine to stress the thoroughly staffed paper as
normal procedure, but in periods of international turmoil the
sense of urgency may require consultation among and quick de-

cisions by top level policy-makers only. This is when the Assistant Secretary steps into the foreground, making decisions—in part at least—on the basis of knowledge previously acquired from desk officers and other subordinates.

RELATING PRACTICE AND THEORY

No matter how excellent the organization nor how well-planned American long-range objectives, the United States is only one among many nations in the United Nations, one among some 180 political entities in the world. The United States has neither the moral influence nor the power to attain a favorable decision, perfect from the American point of view, on every question which troubles relations among states. The degree of success in any given question depends on a staggering number of variables and conditions over which the United States has less than full control. This does not mean the American batting average cannot be improved (nor does it mean that winning a series of cold battles will necessarily bring a cold war to a satisfactory conclusion).

Confronted by a turbulent mid-twentieth century world, with dynamic factors rapidly altering our social and physical relationships, let us assume three broad, long-range goals for American policy—none of which need be incompatible with the reasonable aspirations of other members of the world community: (1) preservation of American national security and a democratic way of life, (2) economic progress and maintenance of, or development toward, political independence for all potentially viable states (without opposing rational movements toward regional unification), and (3) the growth of a democratic order in the relationships between all nations.

The student of social and behavioral disciplines would suggest that within the framework of these goals it might be possible to find policy implementations as specific problems arise which are more likely than other policy alternatives to nudge the world along toward these ends. He has certain theories (or working hypotheses) which might, after careful study by practical policy-makers, be applied on a test basis in limited areas. For example, Gunnar

Myrdal's theory of circular causation [3] spelled out in *Rich Lands and Poor* might be tested by application to the economy of a single cooperating country among those now receiving economic aid from the United States. If the results were encouraging, actually tending to prove more beneficial than present policy at relatively little increase in expense, the policy could be tentatively expanded and retested on a broader base. Thus, hypotheses would be evaluated in the microcosm before billions were wasted or national security was endangered in the macrocosm. In the long run, results might be obtained which practical men did not believe possible (or were afraid to risk on an across-the-board basis) and which would never have been attained if the theory were cast aside without being put to the test. Without bearing a cross for Myrdal's thesis, it serves as an excellent example of the possible application of one theory to a practical situation which remains for the present unsolved.

Recent books by George Kennan, Louis Halle, Charles Burton Marshall, and Dorothy Fosdick [4]—all of whom have served on the Policy Planning Staff in the Department of State—indicate that an ability to integrate practical reality and social or behavioral

[3] Myrdal's theory of circular causation is that an underdeveloped area has low standards of living which result in a poorly educated and relatively unhealthy work force, as well as little working capital for investment. The nature of the labor force causes low production, and producing units already in a country may eventually move to a more favorable location. This further lowers the standard of living, level of education and health, and results in even less investment capital. He calls this the "backwash effect." On the other hand, a country with a relatively high standard of living can maintain or improve its educated and healthy labor force, increasing production, bringing additional funds for investment, and causing additional producing units to enter the area. This he calls the "spread effect." In the first instance, conditions become progressively poorer; in the second, richer. He would be likely to advocate an economic development policy for the United States toward underdeveloped countries which would enable them to turn the corner from regression to progress, from the "backwash effect" to the "spread effect." A policy without sufficient impact to accomplish this goal could never really be successful in making it possible for an underdeveloped country to "go it alone." See Gunnar Myrdal, *Rich Lands and Poor*, New York: Harper and Brothers, 1958.

[4] See Charles Burton Marshall, *The Limits of Foreign Policy*, New York: Henry Holt and Company, 1954; Dorothy Fosdick, *Common Sense and World Affairs*, New York: Harcourt, Brace and Company, 1955; Louis J. Halle, *Choice for Survival*, New York: Harper and Brothers, 1957; George F. Kennan, *Russia, the Atom and the West*, New York: Harper and Brothers, 1958.

theory may be essential in formulating an effective policy leading toward the achievement of reasonable long-range goals. Not all diplomats and policy-makers are conscious of a need to relate theories of international and human relations developed by the social and behavioral disciplines to the resolution of international problems. But, some progress in relating practice and theory is being made at the desk level.

Many young Foreign Service officers and a number of desk men now hold graduate degrees in international relations or allied fields. An FSO may be assigned to a university for language and area training before going to an overseas post; after serving abroad, he may be rotated to the Department as a desk officer. This is not the common practice yet. Most desk officers have had only practical experience in their countries, with no area training before service abroad. When the desk officer completes his tour in the Department, the Foreign Service Institute may send him to a university in mid-career to study the possible contributions of political or economic theory to the making of foreign policy. Later, he may be sent to the National War College, or overseas to its British equivalent, or allowed to attend the Institute's new Senior Officer Course.[5] These opportunities are still the exception rather than the rule.

To academicians, these in-service innovations are steps in the right direction. If there have been failures to coordinate practice and theory in the past, we can at least look forward with some hope. Kennan, Halle, Marshall, and Fosdick are pioneers. Better work may be done in the future.

The desk officer himself may scoff at the need to relate practice and theory, largely because he is so immersed in practical day-to-day operations. Still, how much better it might be if on the occasions when he is drawn into questions of high policy he could comprehend and apply such relationships intuitively under pressure. Certainly not all policy decisions require an understanding of social or behavioral theory, but the long-range implications of the differing philosophies of Dean Acheson and George Kennan,

[5] See discussion on in-service training in Chapter 9.

of John Foster Dulles and Harold Stassen, may stand more clearly revealed to those who can successfully apply such knowledge to contemporary problems.

As the Foreign Service type progresses from the desk to the top rungs of the policy-making ladder, he must become increasingly able to apply both practical and theoretical considerations—common sense and sophisticated concepts—in his analysis of the complex alternatives confronting American foreign policy. For with him may rest the responsibility for decisions which will determine the future of American freedom and democracy for centuries to come; indeed, the fate of Western civilization.

3 Intelligence Analysts
World Weather Forecasters

FUNCTIONS

The more than three hundred intelligence specialists (including sixty-four on country research desks) in the Bureau of Intelligence and Research (INR) of the Department of State are not directly involved in decision-making and operations, as are the country desk officers in the Department's regional bureaus. However, they perform tasks no less essential to the formulation of American foreign policy.

The intelligence analyst is the Department's memory, long-range weather forecaster, theoretician, and human UNIVAC all rolled into one. He provides background information relevant to daily operations, reports facts and analyzes current conditions, interprets trends, and considers possible future developments in every country of the world except the United States. Stated in its most simple form, the function of intelligence research specialists in the Bureau of Intelligence and Research is to present background, facts, and trends on geographic areas and functional topics, so that the formulation and conduct of American foreign and national security policy may rest on a realistic analysis of world conditions.

W. Park Armstrong, Jr., who served for more than ten years as Special Assistant for Intelligence to the Secretary of State, subdivides the general function of the total intelligence operation in the Department into five specific functions:

1. *an alerting function,* calling attention to potential situations which may endanger the national security;

2. *an evaluation function,* sifting and sorting out the unvaluable or undependable information;

3. *an analytical function,* taking the stream of information and studying it in some depth to see what it means for the United States and American foreign policy;

4. *a collection function,* assisting and participating in the processing of raw information and getting it to those who need it; and

5. *an external function,* presenting the politico-socio-economic intelligence viewpoint to other agencies in the intelligence community.[1]

Organization and Personnel

One wag describes the organization of the Bureau of Intelligence and Research (INR) in the Department of State as being structured to perform two functions, one fulfilled by a single Office occupying the bottom two floors of State Annex 1; the other, by six Offices on the top six floors. The information collected on the first two floors, it is said, provides the foundation for the intelligence reports and estimates prepared on the upper six, which invites the conclusion that foreign policy itself is made in Heaven. (This sorry jest will undoubtedly be replaced by another just as bedraggled, as intelligence analysts bid a fond but happy farewell to State Annex 1 and move into the new Department of State Building.) Occupying the lower two floors of the building is the Office of Intelligence Resources and Coordination, which consists of two divisions: (1) Intelligence Collection and Distribution and (2) the Library.

Intelligence Collection and Distribution is the gateway in and out of the Bureau for well over a million documents per month, connecting the Bureau with all the other members of the intelligence community. As our humorist puts it, it collects or gives away

---

[1] For a more detailed discussion of the role of intelligence in decision-making, see Harry Howe Ransom, *Central Intelligence and National Security,* Cambridge, Mass.: Harvard University Press, 1958; Roger Hilsman, *Strategic Intelligence and National Decisions,* Glencoe, Ill.: The Free Press, 1956; Sherman Kent, *Strategic Intelligence for American World Policy,* Princeton, N.J.: Princeton University Press, 1951.

everything that is free (except for what it costs John Q. Public). The Library stocks a collection of about a half-million books and periodicals on international relations and foreign policy (many of which are housed elsewhere and hauled by modern jeep to State Annex 1 for use). It receives regularly issues of some 6,000 periodicals, about two-thirds of which are published abroad. The Library collects what has to be bought.

Occupying the upper six floors of State Annex 1 are six Offices, five geographic and one functional. It is the intelligence analysts who serve within these Offices and their products with which we are most interested. The geographic breakdown by Offices in INR differs somewhat from that in the regional bureaus of the Department, described previously. INR's geographic Offices of Research and Analysis cover: (1) Mid-East and Africa, (2) Western Europe, (3) American Republics, (4) Asia, and (5) the Sino-Soviet Bloc. Within the regional bureaus, a single bureau handles European Affairs, the Near East is combined with South Asian Affairs, and Africa has been promoted in status and is a separate bureau. In the intelligence organization of the Department, the Sino-Soviet Bloc is considered as a region. Attach significance to these interesting differences if you will.

The geographic offices are further subdivided into divisions, which are composed of intelligence analysts serving on country research and on regional political or economic desks. This parallels the compromise between regional and country activities also present within the structure of the regional bureaus of the Department. Insofar as INR can afford the cost, there is at least one desk officer per country, but only 64 desk officers are assigned oversight of some 143 political entities. Only seven desk officers cover the American republics, which averages out to one analyst for three countries, if one does not count regional political and economic analysts. On the other hand, a number of country desk analysts are assigned to cover the Soviet Union and Communist China—enough to make up the better part of an Office. The less information you have on a country of importance, the more effort you must put into squeezing every drop of it out of available material, reading and analyzing every last two-letter word in newspapers and documents. Tiny details have to be pieced together to arrive at tenable conclusions, in much the same fashion as the three blind men who separately touched the trunk, side, and legs of a creature with whom they chanced to cross paths and together were able to determine that they were indeed confronting an elephant.

The Office of Functional and Biographic Intelligence in INR evaluates matters of global concern, including people: commodities like coal, wheat, rice, and oil, or broader questions like economic development, transportation, labor, and communism. It was the Functional Intelligence Division of this Office which, with foresight or luck, had completed a report on traffic through the Suez Canal in October 1956, and could tell who would be affected and how much when the Suez crisis closed the Canal to shipping. That paper was a "popular number." The Biographic Information Division, with its thorough files on government officials and private leaders in countries throughout the world, might be able to help answer satisfactorily one criticism of the Foreign Service implied by *The Ugly American,* that American embassies in Southeast Asia ranked below Soviet embassies in the region in the number or quality of appropriate linguists on their staffs.

Presiding over the Bureau of Intelligence and Research, which is actually composed of eight Offices and twenty-three Divisions, is Hugh Cumming, Director of Intelligence and Research for the Secretary of State. Assisting him in the conduct of his administrative duties is a small Office of the Director, Executive Staff. The Office of Current Intelligence Indications calls his attention to current intelligence information related to daily operations of the Department and undoubtedly staffs some portion of his relations with the Central Intelligence Agency and the inter-departmental Watch Committee. Cumming serves as a direct channel of communication for the Bureau of Intelligence and Research (INR) to the Secretary of State and the Director of Central Intelligence. He is also the direct avenue for guidance to the Bureau by the Secretary or the Director of Central Intelligence. He is the Department's chief representative in the intelligence community, its top-level negotiator in intelligence matters of inter-agency concern.

Exchange of information and the fostering of close relations between research and action officers within the Department of State are fostered at a variety of levels. Intelligence analysts serve on Operations Coordinating Board inter-agency working groups (alongside desk level action officers from the Department's regional bureaus) engaged in specific implementation for OCB of National Security Council policy and in preparing progress reports for OCB and the NSC on operations in the field. Division Chiefs in the Bureau of Intelligence and Research attend the Office Directors' staff and policy meetings in the regional bureaus; INR Office Directors attend the Assistant Secretaries' staff and policy meetings. The Special Assistant to the Director of Intelligence and Research for Reports and Estimates participates regularly in discussions of the Policy Planning Staff. Conversely, action and planning officers attend appropriate research staff discussions.

Wristonization, the integration of Department and field personnel, has been a major concern of the Bureau of Intelligence and Research over the past four years. In the Department's implementation of the Wriston Report,[2] approximately two-thirds of the Bureau's professional positions were classified as dual-service posts,[3] and had to be staffed in the future by Foreign Service officers. Approximately one-third of the Bureau's professional positions remain in civil service categories. Major jobs exempted from Foreign Service assignment are those requiring knowledge of a rare or exotic language. Also exempt are the national intelligence survey editorial and supervisory staffs, in part because of the rigid form and complex directions which must be adhered to in prepara-

[2] For a discussion of the impact of the Wriston Report upon the Department of State, see Chapter 9.

[3] The "dual-service" was the newly integrated Foreign Service, composed both of former Departmental civil service employees and officers already in the Foreign Service. A "dual-service" position may be filled by a civil service employee only if there is no Foreign Service officer available who is qualified to fill the assignment.

tion of the surveys. A small External Research Division, which gathers research from individuals and organizations within the United States on conditions in foreign countries (with a bare nod to the conduct of American foreign policy or international relations), is also exempt. Continuity of relationship is better provided by permanent tenure than by Foreign Service rotation.

The Bureau at first moved slowly but experimentally toward the use of Foreign Service officers. In the past, the Foreign Service has been composed of men interested in operations rather than research. The shift from a civil-service-staffed Bureau to predominant use of Foreign Service personnel could affect adversely the relative emphasis placed upon basic, long-range intelligence reports and estimates, as opposed to operational intelligence. Assignment of middle level Foreign Service personnel as research analysts, even after careful screening, has not always produced satisfactory results. This is partly because Foreign Service officers believe that preferment in their organization is to be gained by service in the regional action bureaus rather than by mastering research positions. Some officers have crystallized as operators and cannot adjust to research. Not even all academic researchers can adapt to the pace and constant pressure of government research.

On the other hand, the Bureau of Intelligence and Research moved with apparent success between 1957 and 1959 to replace civil servants with Foreign Service officers at leadership levels within the Bureau. The present Director, Deputy Director, and Office Directors of the one functional and five regional bureaus producing reports and estimates are now Foreign Service officers. Also in a favorable vein, well over a hundred young Foreign Service officers, Class 8 (the entering category in the Foreign Service), many with graduate degrees, have worked in the Bureau during the past four years as their first assignment after entering the Foreign Service. Their performance has been gratifying, their ability and adaptability remarkable. (Even so, the loss of the old style analysts must have been apparent within the Department.) In the future, as they approach mid-career, it is expected that they will provide a good corps to be drawn on for intelligence assignments in the Department. This trend toward specialization within the Foreign Service, marking the end of a service in which all officers are considered generalists, is likely to be one of the results of Wristonization. If this tends to fragment the Foreign Service itself, it will bind the field and home offices more closely together and make their relations more fruitful.

Assignment of larger numbers of Foreign Service officers to intelligence activities in the Department and integration of some of the civil service analysts into the Foreign Service will help to resolve another problem peculiar to research—staleness. Few men can do basic or operational research day in, day out, year in, year out without losing zest for the job they once loved. Rotation of personnel between field and Department will provide a respite, without losing personnel to jobs outside government.

Integration is likely to reduce seriously the further entry of civil service personnel into research positions for a career in INR. For one thing, opportunities for promotion without transfer to the Foreign Service become vague for civil service employees at the Division Chief level and above. In addition, as integration progresses, the civil servant is likely to be outnumbered and have less in common with his Foreign Service fellow-workers.

Through attrition, the old-type intelligence analyst may eventually pass from the scene, to be replaced by a research type produced by the Foreign Service experience. It is too early to project this new type's characteristics, but it seems that the Bureau of Intelligence and Research will continue to be adequately staffed. On balance, it appears that in the long run more is to be gained than lost as integration progresses.

INTELLIGENCE TYPES

There once was a time, in those economically depressed and relatively uncomplicated years before World War II, when governments placed little emphasis upon intelligence research and analysis. During this drab period the public, in an escapist mood, happily envisioned all intelligence activities as being conducted by two dichotomous types: sinister black-cloaked operatives, with hats pulled low, furtively passing on secrets stolen from foreign governments, or curvaceous sirens, seductively attired in low-cut gowns, lounging on divans in luxuriously appointed drawing rooms, prying security information from unwilling lips. If covert intelligence operations still exist, and it would be naive to assume that what Mata Hari contributed to intelligence is no longer a useful commodity, it is highly unlikely that they are conducted in the flamboyant fashion implied by the public caricature of intelligence types a generation ago.

The modern intelligence type research specialist in the Bureau of Intelligence and Research, who is more Walter Mitty than Herbert Philbrick, undoubtedly has access to whatever covert information is available. But, this much is certain: the research analyst spends more time reviewing materials secured from overt sources than any other.

Attention is centered here on intelligence research and analysis activities in the Department of State, on the coffee and coke rather than the caviar and cocktail level of intelligence operations. The work of the Department's intelligence analysts often consists of dull, plodding research, rather than prodigious feats of derring-do. In short, the intelligence analysts with whom we are concerned get a thrill out of digging in books and periodicals to determine that Communist interest in an off-shore island results from the need for fertilizer to prop up faltering agricultural production rather than from strategic considerations or the discovery of uranium. To them, the act of arriving at this conclusion by research is as exciting as if they had been put ashore from a submarine under cover of darkness and had viewed the actual operations through high-powered binoculars.

It is probably objective young college professor types, patient and persistent, with research ability and a flair for writing, who still find their talents most appreciated at middle levels in the Bureau of Intelligence and Research—men like a former neighbor of mine who is on the French desk—alert, a stimulating conversationalist, full of intellectual curiosity. A fugitive from low classroom salaries, he is a family man and lives on the perimeter of the Washington area in rapidly growing suburbia. On the distaff side, a good-looking red-headed mother of three rides herd on analysts in INR's Office of Research and Analysis for Mid-East and Africa, making their writing succinct, direct and less professorial. She is indeed a *femme fatale,* to endless sentences and reports in which ideas are half hidden by useless detail. Once on the editorial staff of the *Reader's Digest,* she is now the efficient wife of an ex-Foreign Service officer, has lived abroad and worked on an embassy staff.

For the first decade after World War II, the male analyst (in his natural habitat) was seldom a walking advertisement for Brooks Brothers. He was more likely to present the appearance of a professor alone in his study wrestling an idea, with collar loosened and glasses askew. More used to reading documents and reports than to meeting the public, the research analyst was friendly, completely natural, with no professional front. He looked a bit like a balding graduate student, laboring in his tiny nook, with books and manuscripts piled in casual disarray upon a well-used desk. As a matter of fact, his working quarters in a converted apartment house were somewhat more cramped and less comfortable than those available to most graduate students in American universities. This deplorable condition has at last been remedied with the completion of the Department's new building which has risen phoenix-like from an over-sized hole into which State Annex 1 at one time appeared ready to topple.

Within the last few years, Wristonization has replaced almost half of the old-type INR analysts with young Foreign Service officers (most of them just entering the Foreign Service). These new-type analysts may have been selectively winnowed to include only the more studious FSO's, but they look markedly unlike graduate students. (It is amazing how implementation of Wriston's recommendations spruced up costumes in State Annex 1.)

If the old-style civil service intelligence research specialist seemed to belong in an ivory tower, he did not function in one. Neither does the new-style Foreign Service analyst who is fast crowding his predecessor (in some cases now in the Foreign Service and serving overseas) out of the intelligence nest. The Department's excellent communication facilities keep analysts in touch with world developments on an hour-to-hour basis. One has the feeling that the analysts might like to escape the insistence of the pace but are forced by circumstances to meet practical deadlines.

THE SECRETARY'S MORNING BRIEFING

Literally bushels of raw intelligence information flow into INR each day and through the night. The vital essence must be distilled from this mass, without distortion or inaccuracy, and relayed to key officials in the Department.

Briefing officers (one intelligence analyst in each of the five geographic Offices of the Bureau of Intelligence and Research) are responsible by day for following significant international developments. They digest current intelligence items on their respective areas and may consult during the day with a number of other analysts. By 5:00 P.M., each briefing officer discusses the events of the day with his Office Director and adds to his briefing report any evaluation the Director may contribute.

The intelligence analysts serving as briefing officers participate in a dramatic race against time each morning as they boil down the preceding night's take (collating new findings with their summary, prepared in rough draft the afternoon before) for a 9:15 A.M. deadline, the time of the daily briefing session for the Secretary of State and his top advisers.

"Early to bed and early to rise . . ." helps make the heads of government wise. The first alarms go off before 4 A.M. Lights flicker on in suburban homes in Maryland and Virginia as well as the District of Columbia. Monitor room staff members, who work for the Office of Intelligence Resources and Coordination (IRC), begin reporting in about 4:30 A.M.

An Associated Press ticker, turned on by 5 A.M., beats out a drum-fire of news. Another teletype ticks continuously twenty-four hours a day, relaying overseas news and propaganda broadcasts. Fifty feet of intelligence information have rolled in over it since 6 P.M. yesterday. All ticker material is sorted into folders for immediate review by the briefing officers when they arrive.

Sacks containing material which came in during the night to the State Department's communication center are opened and sorted. There are telegrams from embassies and consulates around the globe, messages received by the Central Intelligence Agency, the United States Information Agency, and the military services. You can tell in which areas international tempers are hottest from the size of the stacks building up in the boxes of the briefers.

Analysts assigned to briefing duty begin reporting to the monitoring room shortly before 6:30 A.M. (In time of crisis, it is considerably earlier.) During the winter months, it is scarcely dawn as they arrive. If tensions are high in the Middle East and Eastern Europe, analysts covering these areas are the first to come in. Soon, at least one briefing officer is present from each of INR's area Offices. The briefers pick up the overnight take, sit down at their desks, and start to compare it with information they gathered the preceding afternoon.

The sky brightens outside. The analysts are too busy to notice. They read, sift out less important items, group and reorganize information. More material arrives on their desks as they work. Several typewriters click hesitantly. By 7:15 A.M., the quarters are definitely crowded. Ten or twelve analysts and monitor room staff members are working at nine desks in a room which might comfortably hold four secretaries. As the minutes pass, typewriters tap out a more insistent rhythm. Tension gradually mounts. Briefing reports must be ready between 8:15 and 8:30 P.M. The analysts brief Hugh S. Cumming, Jr., the Director of Intelligence and Research for the Secretary of State, from 8:20 to 9 A.M. He in turn briefs the Secretary and other top-level officials of the Department at 9:15 A.M.

The "master of ceremonies"[4] for the INR briefing of the Director of Intelligence and Research joins analysts in the monitoring room at 7:45 A.M. He glances over their shoulders and men-

[4] The "master of ceremonies" is normally one of the Special Assistants to the Director of Intelligence and Research.

tally picks out the most important topics. At 8:15 A.M., he gathers together the briefing reports and attachments already completed, tears off the latest news summaries, walks quickly to the office of the Director on the third floor of the Department's main building. The Director arrives about 8:00 A.M., or earlier if the international kettle is boiling and is already at work when the "master of ceremonies" arrives. The briefing reports are fanned out on the Director's desk in an orderly sequence. In the next forty minutes he will absorb information in reports produced by almost thirty man-hours of effort.

Hugh Cumming is a Foreign Service officer who assumed his present post after serving as Ambassador to Indonesia, Minister-Counselor in Moscow, and Deputy Secretary-General for Political Affairs of NATO in Paris. He has directed State's intelligence program since 1957, and is the Department's representative on the United States Intelligence Board. His job requires better than average memory, for facts must be retained over long periods and compared on the spur of the moment with contemporary events. Perennial problems fade but may pop up again at any time without warning. Terrorism in Cyprus. Violence in Algeria. Chinese irregular troops on the Burma border. Revolt in Iraq. The Director must carry the historical continuity of these topics and many others in his head, or in a private file always close at hand.

He checks the news summaries first. Then the officer in charge of the briefing indicates the material on the area currently of most importance. The Director reads the reports carefully and glances over the attached background items. The first of the briefing analysts arrives; others will follow; all remain until the briefing comes to a close. They bring additional reports and the late news summaries with them as they complete their activities in the monitoring room.

The Director looks up and asks a question of the Mid-East analyst. The officer-in-charge fits the latest reports arriving from the monitoring room into the material on the desk; he may discard several of lesser importance already there. He keeps one eye on his watch, knows what reports must be seen. The Sino-Soviet

Bloc briefing officer moves up front, then the briefer covering Western Europe. The Director tentatively puts aside an item he had intended to use. Only the most pressing problems can be presented at the Secretary's morning briefing session. Time grows short. He runs over the Asian and Latin American reports. The INR briefing ends on schedule.

The Director has a few minutes alone to review the Department's special summary of incoming and outgoing policy telegrams already digested by Executive Secretariat briefing officers. These officers come in between 3 and 4 A.M., get out their report just before 8:30 A.M. (One early-rising INR briefer assists in the preparation of this summary.) The Secretary is reading the summary in his office on the fifth floor. The Director will avoid duplication but may supplement what he finds there or give a different view if his materials are related to items in the summary.

A minute or two remain to arrange in meaningful order the material he has selected for the morning briefing. In addition to INR briefing reports, he may include an analysis of Communist propaganda trends or a summary of a national intelligence estimate cleared by the United States Intelligence Board but not yet distributed. There may be something of interest from the Watch Committee, a coordinated inter-departmental organization with headquarters in the Pentagon. It is charged with directing a 24-hour-a-day observation of the international scene for indications of the outbreak of hostilities affecting the United States or its principal allies.

With the essential briefing reports and other documents in his hand, precisely at 9:12 A.M., the Director heads down the hall for the Secretary's private elevator, and ascends to the fifth floor. Monday, Wednesday, and Friday, he steps off and enters the Secretary's office, where fifteen to eighteen of the Department's top policy-makers are assembled. On Tuesday and Thursday the briefing session is in an adjoining conference room. About twenty-five to thirty persons are present, including leaders of several other government agencies. Other high officials in the Department are taking their seats as the Director arrives and seats himself at the opposite end of the table from the Secretary of State. The Secretary nods when he is ready.

The Director usually takes five to fifteen minutes to make his oral presentation, covers as many topics, may read excerpts from a speech, an intelligence or military attaché report. He identifies each subject, evaluates the source of his information, gives basic facts and the implications from an intelligence viewpoint. Anyone can interrupt to add information or ask a question. The Secretary follows the briefing intently and often interjects queries. On Tuesdays, the Director is followed by the Director of INR's Office of Research and Analysis for the Sino-Soviet Bloc. The Office Director summarizes political and propaganda developments in Communist bloc countries, including mainland China, but emphasizes the Soviet Union and its European satellites. Then the Secretary gives every person in the room a chance to raise problems for his or others' consideration. There may be general discussion.

The morning briefing normally ends at 9:45 but often runs to 10 A.M. When an international crisis erupts which involves the American national interest, the participants may not get away until 10:30 or 11 A.M. After the meeting, the Director of INR returns to his office and prepares for his subordinates a special précis of information presented at the briefing sessions. In this way, intelligence analysts on briefing duty find out what topics interest the Director and the Secretary and can reintroduce items which seem important but have not yet been used.

The Intelligence Estimate

Not all intelligence activities of INR and the Department proceed at the rapid pace of the briefing operation. Knowledge of current events is necessary, but break-neck speed and an obsession with the contemporary might obscure future problems, and prevent foresight in the formulation of foreign policy. The departmental intelligence estimate adds a forward-looking dimension to the thinking of policy-makers, charts the hidden reefs which may lie over the horizon. It is INR's real glamour product and may be its most important single contribution to national security.

Man has been seeking to predict the future since long before the days of Nostradamus. Intelligence analysts deny that they predict but admit that they project what the future may be, assuming that certain conditions remain unchanged or that certain trends continue. The INR estimates group has hammered out more than eighty-seven intelligence estimates for the Department. It also develops basic drafts of political, economic, and sociological information included in the national intelligence estimates published (for government use only) by the Central Intelligence Agency.

The estimates group looks two, five, even ten years ahead. On one occasion, it is said, the group attempted to envision the population and economic conditions of one particular continent in the year 2000 A.D. Chairman of the group is Allan Evans, Special Assistant to the Director (of INR) for Reports and Estimates. Other members are the Directors of INR's one functional and five regional Offices. (But first drafts of any estimates the group considers are prepared by intelligence research analysts at the country desk level.)

Dr. Evans presides in genial fashion over group discussions held twice weekly in his office, encourages discussion and dissent. An objective scholar and former member of the faculty at Harvard University, he entered intelligence during World War II, served four years with the Office of Strategic Services in London under the late "Wild Bill" Donovan, who pioneered the modern American intelligence service. No one understands better than Evans the necessity of trying to project international behavior, nor has greater realization of the limitations of the social sciences at their present level of development. He has guided intelligence research and analysis in INR since 1946, and is admirably fitted to direct the application of social theory to practical problems affecting the development of foreign governments.

What will be the results of Russian economic penetration in the underdeveloped countries of the world? A question such as this may be asked by an Assistant Secretary or an Office Director in a regional action bureau of the State Department. An intelligence estimate is always triggered by a problem. The question must be refined, assumptions spelled out. The answer may be based on a continuation of present policies or upon actions hypothesized for the future. The estimates group determines the terms of reference within which the problem will be attacked. At this point, analysts in one or more of INR's Offices are asked to write first drafts of an estimate. The products are circulated among the estimates group members.

In discussions, the Office Directors play the role of universal scholars. Formerly civil servants and chosen for their knowledge of a special field and the breadth of their interests in other areas of the social sciences, they are now all Foreign Service officers. The best ideas from the rough drafts are combined. The resulting paper is rewritten page by page and word by word. Intelligence analysts who wrote drafts are consulted as work progresses. It once took the estimates group eleven two-hour sessions to produce an approved estimate.

An intelligence estimate is from two to forty pages in length. It opens with a statement of the problem. Then come the conclusions in four to eight numbered paragraphs. This is all most busy policy-makers have time to read. For those directly responsible for making decisions on the problem, the background thinking of the estimates group is included. The present situation and recent developments are noted. There is an analysis of domestic affairs in the foreign area and a consideration of future prospects. This is the foundation which may affect foreign relations. Finally, the area's current foreign policy goals and operations as well as possible future activities are analyzed. Detailed research papers on political or economic phases of the problem are appended. Copies of estimates and attachments go to Hugh Cumming, to leading Department policy-makers, and to members of the Policy Planning Staff, and are forwarded to the Central Intelligence Agency.

OTHER INTELLIGENCE PRODUCTS

The day-to-day bread and butter work of INR for the Department is incorporated in intelligence reports and intelligence briefs. The main distinction between the two is one of size. This involves the question of how much detail can be included and how broad a topic covered. Reports are five or more pages in length and may run to several hundred. Briefs are four pages or less. Reports and briefs bear some resemblance to intelligence estimates but are less rigid in form. They are cleared at the Office level within INR, sent to officers in the Department or other government agencies.[5]

The Bureau of Intelligence and Research prints two classified periodicals of interest to Department policy-makers and other government officials but not available to the public. *Soviet Affairs* deals with the Soviet Union and the satellites; *International Communism* discusses developments in Communist parties and movements outside the Soviet bloc.

Some of the most useful information for daily operations in the Department is provided by the Biographic Information Division of the Office of Functional and Biographic Intelligence. Biographic reports, which range from ten to forty pages in length, are seldom dull; they contain information on the political, economic, and cultural leaders of every country in the world except the United States. Not only are people likely to be more interesting than abstractions like governments or economies, but also in diplomacy it pays to "know thy enemy" and to "know thy friend." A negotiator at an international conference can be more effective if he knows the people sitting across from him, their fundamental beliefs about the country they represent and about the United States, and their personal likes and dislikes.

The country desk officer in a regional bureau makes a quick assessment if a cabinet falls abroad, or when government leaders or ambassadors are replaced. (For example, Mikhail A. Menshikov, the Soviet ambassador to the United States, spent most of his previous government career specializing in trade problems; would he put more emphasis on developing trade relations?) What new

[5] A considerable portion of the intelligence research papers prepared have a multiple distribution and are not prepared to meet the needs of a particular individual or desk. The Bureau cannot be certain how useful such reports are or to what use they are put. In view of the avalanche of paper flowing through the Department, less use of broadcast materials and more emphasis upon papers to meet special needs might be a useful redirection of effort.

emphases are there likely to be in the country's domestic or foreign policies? What should be the American reaction to the change?

Intelligence information prepared essentially for the use of the Department is packaged in a wide variety of forms and serves many purposes. It is in daily use by policy-makers at every level in the Department of State, from the desk officer to the Secretary himself. A big user of INR reports and estimates is the Department's Policy Planning Staff, which keeps a watchful eye on the preparation of Department position papers for consideration by the National Security Council Planning Board and which is responsible for briefing the Secretary for meetings of the National Security Council. It has no research staff of its own and relies on INR facilities.

RELATIONS WITH THE CIA-NSC-OCB COMPLEX

The intelligence analysts in the Bureau of Intelligence and Research, like Janus, actually face two ways—they service the internal needs of the Department of State, and cooperate with the Washington intelligence community to serve the Central Intelligence Agency, the National Security Council, and the Operations Coordinating Board, which reposes within the National Security Council structure in half-digested state.

The INR analysts are responsible for injecting political, economic, and sociological facts on foreign countries or global functional problems into the flow of intelligence information reaching the Central Intelligence Agency. Other government intelligence agencies emphasize other factors, exchanging information among themselves and with CIA to prevent unnecessary duplication of effort.

INR analysts contribute elements of two Central Intelligence Agency products used extensively by the National Security Council, and probably by some other government departments and agencies: the national intelligence estimate and the national intelligence survey. Remember how the intelligence estimate was triggered for Department use? If the same question were raised at some level within the National Security Council machinery (at a meeting of the Planning Board Assistants, the Planning Board, or the National Security Council itself) or required a broad collation of views (including those of the military), it seems likely that the Central Intelligence Agency would assume leadership in the formulation of a national intelligence estimate.

The operations and organization of the Central Intelligence Agency remain one of Washington's best kept "secrets." Published facts for tracing the procedures used in developing national intelligence estimates are as scarce as hen's teeth. But in the realm of public knowledge are several clues which provide some basis for an "educated guess" as to what goes on during the preparation of a national estimate.

To begin with, as important and powerful as the Central Intelligence Agency may be, like other governmental mechanisms, it is organized and operated by men—intelligent men to be sure, but trained as administrators and organizers in the same universities as those who function in other agencies of government. And it is part of the over-all government organization responsible for the development of national security policy. A political scientist will be pardoned the observation that government procedures for clearance and coordination may vary in detail—the names of the participating agencies may change—but procedures of clearance and coordination are pretty much the same throughout the executive branch of the government (at least in those segments exposed to the public gaze).

John W. Evans, former Deputy Director of the Office of Intelligence Research in the Department of State, writing in the *Foreign Service Journal* of March, 1957, says that OIR, once the major portion of what is now INR, "produces both its own [intelligence] estimates and the Department's contributions to national intelligence estimates. The latter are the joint product of the intelligence community and are finally accepted and authorized by the Intelligence Advisory Committee [now called the United States Intelligence Board], on which . . . [the Director of Intelligence and Research] is the Department's member. As the intelligence foundation for decisions of the NSC, these estimates play a decisive role in the formulation of the policy decisions of the U.S. government in the field of national security."

Let us project, on the basis of this knowledge and other material which has since entered the public realm, what can be hypothesized or known. Apparently, the United States Intelligence Board is composed of the heads of major intelligence agencies. These include CIA, State, Army, Navy, Air Force, the Joint Chiefs of Staff, the Federal Bureau of Investigation, and perhaps even the Atomic Energy Commission. Allen Dulles, the Director of Central Intelligence, chairs meetings of the USIB (because of CIA's role as leader of the intelligence community).

A national estimate—from whatever level or source requested —will not be developed until the project has been authorized by the USIB. In like manner, a proposed national estimate does not become the basis for government action until it has been approved by the USIB. In government, whenever an inter-agency group must authorize development of a paper like the national estimate, the staff of some agency or a subordinate inter-agency group must be responsible for drawing up a statement of the problem with which the paper is to deal and the terms of reference to lower-level inter-agency groups or to department staffs who will do the actual drafting of the paper.

Because of the veil drawn over procedures by which the national estimates are developed, the Central Intelligence Agency certainly plays a key role. The existence of an estimates group in the Department of State indicates that the Department and other agencies also take an important part in the development of national estimates. The Office of National Estimates of CIA (which is the agency best fitted to serve as a staff arm of the USIB since the Director of Central Intelligence is its chairman) guides the clearance and coordination process and contributes substantially to the drafting of national estimates. In like manner, it appears that within State the estimates group (and other INR intelligence analysts) would be active in producing tentative drafts of portions of such an estimate. It is said that State's contribution is blended into a composite draft of a national estimate by the Office of National Estimates, subject to review by the Board of National Estimates of CIA.

Unless the intelligence community operates in ways alien to typical government patterns, the blending of estimates in a number of fields produced by a variety of agencies requires at some point a process of discussion and accommodation. Lower-level inter-agency working groups (at Division or Office levels) make revisions of tentative composite drafts, or beat out such agreement as possible, before later drafts are submitted to the USIB for consideration and final approval.

If intelligence estimates are typical inter-departmental products, agency heads on USIB can reserve positions in footnotes on matters where complete agreement cannot be achieved. This would serve as a warning to the National Security Council and its staff, and would enable decisions at the NSC level based upon such estimates to allow for the possibility that the dissenter was not entirely incorrect.

Evaluation of the validity of national estimates from time to time would be a proper function of the USIB or its backstop organization in CIA. As events progress on the international scene, previous estimates could be compared with new estimates as a means of pointing out what defects time has revealed in the originals. In addition, if this is not already done, agencies could be required to assess the adequacy of the information upon which they based their contributions to the national estimate and could indicate the facts still needed.

As in the case of the preparation of policy papers for the National Security Council, intelligence estimates must demand extra effort and are likely to be reserved for topics of greatest importance. Complex procedures of discussion and clearance, while necessary, are probably a drain on the time and energy of participating personnel.

A national intelligence survey, another intelligence product, discussed at some length in John Evans' *Foreign Service Journal* article, requires painstaking research. These surveys may take up to one-half of INR's time and personnel and are of tremendous importance to the Department and to the intelligence community.

Evans writes of the national intelligence surveys, "Each of the individual chapters on each country represents a major project in research and exposition. In this vast undertaking, the Department, with the benefit of reports from foreign missions and of other sources . . . [in the Bureau of Intelligence and Research], is responsible for the chapters on political, sociological, and a considerable portion of economic affairs. A few chapters, such as that on the country's geography or its weather, may stand for years, but in the fields of State's responsibility, fundamental changes occur in many countries quite rapidly, so that revised editions of its chapters are constantly required."

He continues by saying, "At the present stage of the program almost 50 per cent of the total production effort is being devoted to work on revising chapters previously published. While more than half of the chapters for many countries have yet to be written, all have been published for most countries of major importance, and the total library of printed NIS's represents a tremendously valuable fund of basic intelligence for the use of the Foreign Service officer."

What is the purpose of the national intelligence surveys? Evans declares, "The objective is to develop and put into usable, consistent form—and to keep up to date—a comprehensive analysis of all the information about each foreign country that may be needed for future planning decisions of the U.S. government."

If State contributes only a portion of the chapters in the national intelligence surveys, other agencies gather and draft additional chapters. Since the procedures of formulating national surveys have not been more fully described (and since the CIA is the chief intelligence agency of the government), it is realistic to ascribe leadership in the preparation or reproduction of national intelligence surveys to the Office of National Surveys in the Central Intelligence Agency.

Various members of the intelligence community apparently

cooperate under CIA leadership to prepare a joint product. One may venture a guess, rightly or wrongly, that the factual nature of the national surveys places considerable responsibility upon each participating agency for the substantive detail included in its chapters. This would require less inter-agency coordination than the development of a national estimate, perhaps more careful supervision within each agency.

No practical observer of government would assume that the intelligence community goes to all the trouble of producing national intelligence surveys for fun. It is clear that descriptions in national surveys are not namby-pamby accounts of formal organization and will not be limited to discussion of surface conditions in the countries analyzed. They are more likely to offer penetrating insights into the actual functioning of a government.

For example, the discussion of election processes may not be limited to formal processes but probably includes the way elections are rigged and manipulated. Thus, Foreign Service officers at posts overseas may be alerted to such possibilities, and watch behind-the-scene developments carefully. Country desk officers in the action bureaus of the Department, if forewarned, can make plans to adjust American foreign policy to a new situation. Review of National Security Council policies can be initiated if changes are likely to alter a situation substantially and consideration of new alternatives becomes a necessity.

CONCLUSIONS

Three major questions arise in the performance of the intelligence function by the Bureau of Intelligence and Research of the Department of State. At what levels should intelligence information be introduced into the policy-making stream? What should be the role of the intelligence analyst as a participant in Department meetings for consideration of policy questions? What should be the relationship of the Bureau in the Department to the Central Intelligence Agency and other members of the intelligence community?

Since the establishment of the Bureau of Intelligence and Research in 1946, many suggestions have been made of ways to increase the usefulness of intelligence operations to policy-makers. It has been argued that intelligence analysts should gather information and make policy decisions themselves, that centralized intelligence operations should be broken up and intelligence analysts attached to action bureaus of the Department, and that intelligence information should not be introduced into the policy process until questions reach the Secretary of State.

To the outsider looking in, it would appear that an independent intelligence organization, injecting intelligence information at all levels in policy-making, and at each successive stage in the consideration of policy, is the only practical means by which Department of State decision-makers can be forced to focus at all times upon practical policy alternatives, to adjust to dynamic, ever-changing situations.

Decision-makers may become emotionally bound up in their own decisions, defend policies long after they have served their useful purposes, become immersed in tactical considerations, or forget the relationship of tactics to long-range strategy. The intelligence analysts must have no interest in defending a policy because it exists, must pull no punches if he feels it runs counter to fundamental needs or basic trends. It is not his role to wrestle with how to handle the transition to a new policy, except as he analyzes the possible effect of proposed actions upon the areas or problems involved.

There is a fine line between policy-making and analysis of what the effects of policy will be; the latter may influence the former to such an extent that analysis—to all intents and purposes—becomes active policy-making. To the young Foreign Service officer serving as an intelligence analyst on policy committees with fellow Foreign Service officers from the regional bureaus this will be a provocative line, over which he is likely to step on occasion, with peril to the proper performance of the intelligence function. This danger may require constant patrolling at all levels to prevent any further growth of the involvement of analysts in policy-making, to preserve some detachment and less interest in policy than in the facts themselves.

Department policy-makers sometimes tend to reject intelligence information, because they view it as undermining a policy with which they feel a personal identification; such identification on the part of the intelligence analyst would be even more tragic. There will be no more curative influence upon American foreign policy than the continued injection of objective analysis by an independent intelligence organization at every level in the policy-making process within the Department of State.

The relationship between CIA and the Bureau of Intelligence and Research in the Department of State, and of CIA with other departments or agencies of government, has evolved over a period of time into a balance between complete centralization of the performance of the intelligence function by CIA and complete decentralization or compartmentalization of the function in individual departments or agencies. That such a compromise between extremes exists is evident from the description of the Bureau's internal functions and of its relationship to the CIA–NSC–OCB complex.

The major argument for centralization is simply that the Central Intelligence Agency is in a better position to assess all the facts and put them into a balanced perspective than any single department or agency. The strongest argument for decentralization is that individual agencies are in a better position to know what information they need and to tailor their products to suit their particular needs. The reason that the present compromise arrangement has proven more acceptable than the extreme alternatives is that the advantages of the extremes are not lost by maintaining both a Central Intelligence Agency and individual intelligence components in the executive departments and agencies.

With the present form of organization, agencies like State can develop their independent views and service their individual needs, but they are subject to the cross-check of composite analyses evolved by Central Intelligence Agency leadership and coordina-

tion of the intelligence community. In reverse, the individual intelligence services remain a cross-check upon the blended analyses
of the Central Intelligence Agency and can "red-flag" differences
of opinion so that top policy-makers are aware of possible errors.
While there may be fluctuations in the balance between the Central Intelligence Agency and the components of the intelligence
community, there is no reason to believe that a decided move in
either direction from the present situation would improve the quality of the intelligence information available to decision-makers
or meet as well the variety of needs which must be serviced.[6]

In a quiet and not always publicly discernible way, the day-to-
day implementation of the intelligence function by analysts in
the Bureau of Intelligence and Research is affecting tremendously
the survival of freedom and democracy. Their work is a constructive force in the formulation and conduct of American foreign
policy and is not destined to fade away. But it must continue to
be coordinated with the labors of analysts in other agencies, so
that the whole intelligence community can benefit from the products of each of its parts. If the balance is sometimes uneasy, it is
no less necessary.

[6] For a delightful yet serious exploration of the major problems relating intelligence to policy formation, see Allan Evans, "Intelligence and Policy Formation," *World Politics,* October 1959, pp. 84–91.

4 Policy-Planners
Men of Practical Vision

FUNCTIONS

The eleven members of the Policy Planning Staff of the Department of State—unlike the country desk officers and the intelligence analysts—are excused from day-to-day decision-making and operations, and from original research to find facts and project trends.[1] Even so, the position of America in the world a decade from now depends in large measure on how successfully their deliberations are blended into the mainstream of Department operations and policy-making.

The primary function of the desk officer is operational, with limited participation in the National Security Council machinery which grinds out longer-range policies. The task of the intelligence analyst is equitably divided between operational intelligence and estimates of future conditions, but he is pledged to abstain from policy-making (although he sometimes falls off the wagon).

The policy-planner backstops the Secretary of State as he takes part in the formulation of broad National Security Council policies and advises him on operations only in those moments, which now

---

[1] As of April 1, 1959, there were ten planners, including the Assistant Secretary, who also bore the titles of Director of Policy Planning and Department Representative on the NSC Planning Board. There was a Deputy Assistant Secretary who served as an alter ego to the Assistant Secretary. In addition, one member of the Planning Staff was designated as NSC Planning Board Alternate and another as Executive Secretary of the Planning Staff. Two of the remaining six members divided the task of representation of the department at meetings of the NSC Planning Board Assistants. An eleventh member has been added to the Planning Staff to handle the Board Assistants' work on a full-time basis, relieving two members for more reflective duties.

seem to come rather often, when crucial decisions may alter our basic relationships with a disturbed, dynamic world.

The desk officer is an operator; the intelligence analyst, a fact-projector; the policy-planner, a thoughtful overseer and a man of practical vision. As the appointed integrator of future needs with present realities, the planner was to show the way at major policy crossroads, and to lead the nation toward the achievement of its long-term goals and interests. This was a big order, and not all Secretaries have asked that it be filled.

The essential task of the Policy Planning Staff is the collection of factual material, and the preparation and discussion of policy studies, followed by long-range recommendations to top decision-makers. Because of the Staff's limited physical resources, it studies only the most basic issues, usually leaving day-to-day decisions to the Assistant Secretaries or other policy-making officers in the regional and functional bureaus. It has shunned, insofar as possible, consideration of matters of only transitory operational significance.

Department Order No. 393 of May 8, 1947, which established the Staff, stated its five major functions as follows:

1. formulating and developing, for the consideration and approval of appropriate officials of the Department, long-term programs for the achievement of U.S. foreign policy objectives;

2. anticipating problems which the Department may encounter in the discharge of its mission;

3. undertaking studies and preparing reports on broad politico-military problems;

4. examining problems and developments affecting U.S. foreign policy in order to evaluate the adequacy of current policy and making advisory recommendations on them; and

5. coordinating planning activities within the Department of State.

This is said to constitute as good a statement of Policy Planning Staff functions today as it did in 1947.

Given birth by Secretary of State George C. Marshall, who confronted his brainchild in its infancy with the gigantic task of "planning" the European economic recovery program, the Policy Planning Staff enjoyed a brief spate of publicity which gave promise of a continuing blow-by-blow description of policy-advisers facing life and the future. After this grand opening, the Policy Planning Staff—so far as the general public was concerned— retired to anonymity and obscurity, from which it has seldom emerged. Its disappearance from public view and its separation from the shifting winds of public opinion and political pressure were essential to the performance of the role for which the Staff was conceived.

The Mr. X article on "The Sources of Soviet Conduct" in the July 1947 issue of *Foreign Affairs* was the conceptual framework within which the planners functioned in those early days. Authored by George F. Kennan, the Policy Planning Staff's distinguished first director, it spelled out the assumptions and aims of our post-World War II policy toward the Soviet Union. Kennan's "containment" thesis became the guiding principle of American strategy. Under his leadership in those first creative days, the planners sought to add perspective to foreign policy, to eliminate inconsistencies, to develop a broad regional and even global view.

When Marshall retired, Kennan stayed on as Director of Policy Planning under Secretary of State Dean Acheson. Sometimes Acheson walked in quietly from his office adjoining the Staff conference room to take part in the discussions. He found this exchange of ideas with the planners extremely valuable at such a critical time— the post-war period of increasing Soviet-American tension, of determining the degree of American involvement and commitment in world affairs, of continued struggle to adjust to the harsh demands of leadership.

The need for the Policy Planning Staff remains today. Policy evolved from the desk level upward runs the risk of precipitating a series of accommodations among equals, between two offices within a bureau, and between two bureaus. There is a tendency to split differences, to come up with a watery compromise lacking the perceptive originality which would give the policy seaworthiness, and allow it to remain afloat in the stormy seas of international controversy.

The Assistant Secretaries of State are too often exhausted from the deadly undertow of daily crisis which draws them down to consideration of minute detail. Confronted by an endless series of issues and problems rolling into the Department via cable, they are rarely able to lift their thoughts, and to contemplate grand relationships. It is left to the planners—disengaged from routine policy-making—to help chart the Secretary of State's route without losing sight of the strategic course for the dangerous years ahead.

PERSONNEL

More than sixty-five persons, including its four directors, have served on the Policy Planning Staff since its founding in 1947. Membership on the staff is highly prized. Selection has been on the basis of "intellectual capacity, a sense of responsibility, and the ability to work in harmony with others." Economists and area specialists have been blended with men of general competence in foreign affairs.

At times, Foreign Service officers have dominated the membership of the Policy Planning Staff. Although the present policy is to preserve a balance between the Foreign Service and appointees from positions in private life, the Policy Planning Staff in 1959 included four Foreign Service officers; four long-time Department employees, and only two members from the "outside." The personnel records of Foreign Service officers to be promoted to the staff are thoroughly studied before appointment is made. Indications of lack of initiative or of superficiality would be disqualifying. Appointees from private life are equally carefully screened. It is doubtful if any of them have been asked to serve on the Policy Planning Staff primarily because of political considerations, although some few appointees have come from "good" political families.

In the five years following 1947, staff changes brought an average of seven new members onto the Policy Planning Staff per year. The changing of party control in the executive branch in 1953 had no appreciable effect on the number rotated, as only seven new members were appointed; but several of those who stepped aside did so for political reasons. Between 1953 and 1958, changes averaged only three per year. The slower speed of rotation may be indicative of the more specialized and technical nature of the work of the Policy Planning Staff as it adjusted to the National Security Council procedures and engaged in less wide-ranging discussion of broad policy considerations. A single individual—no matter how intelligent—is likely to be useful longer as a technical expert than as an idea man.

In the early years, the personnel policy on rotation consisted of "picking a man's brains" for his ideas until you had learned all he knew. Then you sent him on. Although it would be unfair to attribute rapid rotation only to an absence of ideas, many members survived less than one year. The average period was under two years. That Dorothy Fosdick, the only woman ever appointed to the Staff, served more than four years—from 1949 to 1953—indicates the breadth of her abilities and the scope of her contributions to the work of the Policy Planning Staff.

At least six new appointments to the Policy Planning Staff were made in 1958. Robert Bowie, of course, had resigned as Director of the Staff, but it is difficult to attribute any single cause to this upsurge. It seems likely that the impact of the successful launching of the Soviet sputniks and the development of inter-continental missiles capable of delivering atomic or hydrogen warheads had some effect. Gerard Smith became Director of the Policy Planning Staff in 1958 after four years in the Department as Special Assistant to the Secretary for Atomic Energy Affairs. Before entering the Department, he had served four years as a Special Assistant to Commissioner Thomas E. Murray of the Atomic Energy Commission.

There is a need once more for broad, courageous thinking by members of the Policy Planning Staff. (Fortunately, some policy-planners seem to be aware of this fact.) The dynamic characteristics of the national security situation may have shattered the somewhat conservative and routine approach to foreign policy which the maturing NSC machinery and the mild leadership of the Eisenhower administration tended to encourage.

If some members of the Policy Planning Staff left their mark upon certain aspects of American foreign policy, the experience of serving on the Staff had a reciprocal effect upon their thinking and the methods by which they now approach policy problems. This is evident in books produced by four of the early members of the Staff after retirement into private life. Kennan has proliferated his ideas in multiple publications, including *American Diplomacy, 1900–1950; Realities of American Foreign Policy;* and *Russia, the Atom and the West.* Charles Burton Marshall's *The Limits of Foreign Policy* was followed by Dorothy Fosdick's *Common Sense and World Affairs,* and by Louis J. Halle's *Civilization and Foreign Policy* and *Choice for Survival.*

If there is a common way of thinking about policy in these books, it lies in recognition that there are definite limits to what America can do at any given time and place, in a tolerance of differing ideas and cultures among the peoples of the world, and in an appreciation of the relationship of high theory to practical policy. Implicit in their writings is the concept of an integrative and adaptive foreign policy, consisting of political, military, economic, and informational aspects, ever searching for some degree of consistency between short-run implementations and long-range goals. The Policy Planning Staff experience permeates many paragraphs of these perceptive works as well as those of periodical articles produced by other former planners.

SOURCES OF INFORMATION

Members of the Policy Planning Staff may be separated from the nagging duties of daily operations, but they do not enjoy splendid isolation or work in an ivory tower. Operational information from the policy-makers and studies from the intelligence analysts (or from researchers in the Historical Office) reach them regularly and in abundance. The information resources of the entire government are at their beck and call.

Would they like to talk with a desk officer or an Assistant Secretary, with the Legal Adviser, or with an expert in diplomatic or world history, such as William L. Langer or Arnold Toynbee? He is invited to consult. Would they like to explore problems of economic development with a private scholar or government expert? He will respond. Their problem is one of selection, but keeping abreast of the Department's daily operations is in itself a sizable chore.

When the Assistant Secretary for Policy Planning (Director of the Policy Planning Staff) comes in at 8:45 each morning, he finds on his desk the *Daily Staff Summary*, prepared by duty officers from the Publications Section of the Executive Secretariat who reported to the Department between 3 and 4 A.M. Only twenty-four Department officers receive this summary. It is a four- to five-page précis of the most important policy cables reaching the Department during the night. It includes a "Staff Record" which lists all decisions made the previous day by the Secretary of State, the Under Secretary, the Under Secretary for Political Affairs, and the Deputy Under Secretary for Administration. Circulated with the summary are unclassified news reports from the Department's three press association tickers in the Office of News in the Bureau of Public Affairs.

At 9:15 A.M. each day, the Assistant Secretary walks down the hall to the Secretary of State's regular staff conference, attended by all top leaders of the Department with the rank equivalent to Assistant Secretary and above. The group receives an intelligence briefing each morning from the Director for Intelligence and Research. After this analysis, operational problems are raised by any of the participants (especially the Assistant Secretaries from the regional bureaus) and discussed by those present.

Several times a week, the policy-planners attend staff meetings in the various regional or functional bureaus of the Department. These either precede the Secretary's morning staff meeting or immediately follow it. Anything of particular importance learned in this round of early morning meetings can be exchanged at the Policy Planning Staff's own daily half-hour briefing session at 10:15 A.M. With this background of information, they are ready to begin the day's work.

By 1:30 P.M., the members of the Policy Planning Staff and the Director receive three copies of Department's *Daily Secret Summary,* prepared by public affairs officers in the geographic bureaus of the Department. It goes to approximately 130 Department officers. (Country desk officers receive only the sections related to their own bureaus.) Accompanying this summary are the *Daily Opinion Summary* by the Public Opinion Studies Staff of the Bureau of Public Affairs and a brief legislative report from the Congressional Relations Area.

By 3:00 P.M., the Assistant Secretary receives the *Afternoon Staff Summary,* in effect a continuation of the *Daily Staff Summary* issued at 8:45 A.M. It is usually six or seven pages in length, and includes on its final page a "Record of Actions," indicating major decisions taken by the Assistant Secretaries and Special Assistants of equivalent rank during the past twenty-four hours. Circulated with it is the *Daily Legislative Summary* from the Congressional Relations Area. The Assistant Secretary may communicate useful information from the *Staff Summary* to interested policy-planners. In addition, memoranda or policy statements in the process of development in the bureaus are routed to policy-planners for information purposes. Particularly significant reports from embassies in the field may also come across their desks.

If the policy-planners have a close relationship to daily operations in the Department, they are even more dependent upon information received from intelligence sources for the successful performance of their essential duties. The facts and projections from these studies provide the necessary detachment from daily events and the proper perspective for the development of longer-range policy suggestions. The Bureau of Intelligence and Research of the Department of State is the research backstop for the Policy

Planning Staff. The relationship is so close, the reliance on research so complete, that the Special Assistant to the Director (of INR) for Reports and Estimates and an appropriate Office Director attend most meetings of the Policy Planning Staff.

Intelligence estimates, reports, and briefs are furnished to the policy-planners as requested, sometimes even prepared and forwarded before the planners themselves are aware of the need for them. Because of INR's cooperation with other members of the intelligence community in Washington, it can make available to the policy-planners any type of intelligence information, military or otherwise, including material from national intelligence estimates or national intelligence surveys prepared cooperatively under the direction of the Central Intelligence Agency.

Any one of the Department's five regional bureaus (European, Inter-American, Near Eastern and South Asian, African, or Far Eastern Affairs) may be asked to send a representative to a policy-planning discussion. A specialist from the Bureau of Economic Affairs or the Bureau of International Organization Affairs may be present.[2]

The Policy Planning Staff often calls in a government or Department official (such as Henry Cabot Lodge or Francis O. Wilcox) or sometimes a private individual possessing knowledge which will be of particular value in resolving the problem with which it is dealing. Former directors of the Staff, like Kennan, Paul H. Nitze, or Robert R. Bowie (all now engaged in academic pursuits) may return to talk with the policy-planners. A useful weekly meet-

[2] The Bureau of Economic Affairs is considered to be a functional bureau. Actually this Bureau serves in an advisory capacity to the regional bureaus on economic questions of a regional or local character but may have action responsibility in determining economic policy on a global or inter-regional basis, subject to consultation and advice from the regional bureaus. An economic question arising in the United Nations would become the action responsibility of the Bureau of International Organization Affairs.

If a question which has been handled by one of the other regional bureaus is placed on the agenda of a United Nations organ, action responsibility for the item shifts from the original regional bureau to the Bureau of International Organization Affairs. Action responsibility for questions coming before the Organization of American States, however, resides in the Bureau of Inter-American Affairs.

ing with the "joint staff" of the Joint Chiefs of Staff provides an off-the-record exchange of ideas between the Policy Planning Staff and the military.

The best in commentary from the domestic and foreign press is likely to reach the policy-planners. If another Mr. X article (or one less significant) appears, they will read it as a matter of course. Books like Henry Kissinger's *Nuclear Weapons and Foreign Policy* are on the shelves in their conference room. They have been thoroughly read. Even though planners sometimes "get up to their necks" in work during a period of crisis, normally they do have sufficient time to read periodicals and books.

OPERATIONS

Although the members of the Policy Planning Staff spend most of their time in individual offices just down the corridor from those of the Under Secretary and Secretary, the nature of their operations leads one to visualize them most often grouped around the large mahogany table in their conference room attempting to arrive at a consensus under the leadership of the Assistant Secretary for Policy Planning.

The conference room is simple, almost austere, in keeping with the intellectual approach of the policy-planners. It appears functional, is appropriately furnished. Comfortable leather chairs surround the long table. Books line parts of two walls; a gigantic map of the world, a third; a row of windows, the fourth. There are neither telephones nor incoming and outgoing baskets. These, of course, are the trademarks of the offices in the operating bureaus. The only objects on the table are a simple pad and pencil in front of each chair, typical arrangements for staff meetings throughout the Department and government.

The amount of use the conference room gets has varied widely through the years. As one policy-planner has said, "It doesn't pay to meet just to meet." Kennan gathered the staff together almost daily for group discussions. Bowie, on the other hand, preferred individual talks with members of his staff. A week might go by without general discussion. Twice a week is considered the normal pattern, with meetings scheduled on Tuesday mornings from 10 to 12 and on Thursday afternoons from 2 to 5. In time of crisis, the Staff has been in almost continuous session for twenty-four hours.

Questions are placed on the agenda of the Policy Planning Staff at the request of the Secretary of State to resolve a purely Departmental problem, or stem from matters discussed at some level within the National Security Council structure. Consideration of problems may be initiated by the Director or one of the policy-planners. Confronted by a problem situation, the policy-planners must define the question which needs to be answered and determine how to go about their work. The collection and digestion of written information is supplemented in informal discussions with operating officers or intelligence analysts in the Department. A formal meeting of the policy-planners may be held to receive a briefing from experts or to discuss with Department officers or outside specialists the full range of implications in the situation under review. The Planning Staff then meets alone to reach a consensus among its own members, to evolve informal agreement on a common policy.

The policy-planner best fitted by experience and field of knowledge is usually assigned to coordinate the drafting of a policy paper (either on a contemporary problem or of the longer-range "think piece" variety which discusses long-range trends and their general application for American foreign policy). The paper may be based in part on a memorandum prepared by a desk officer (much of the detailed drafting must be done at this level) and on the report of an intelligence analyst (or on a national intelligence estimate). The product is circulated among the members of the Staff and to other officers in the Department. As the criticisms come in, the paper is reviewed and edited. Once accord is reached on a revised draft of a paper prepared for the Secretary, either at his request or upon the initiative of the Staff,[3] the policy paper

---

[3] The emphasis was upon the latter during the tenure of Secretary of State Dulles, especially with regard to "think pieces" prepared for use outside the NSC structure.

is forwarded to the Secretary after being reviewed rather casually by the Executive Secretariat. Policy Planning papers primarily for use within the Department have no standard form. ("Think piece" papers are not checked by the Executive Secretariat for clearances as is the case with most if not all other Department policy papers.) They may start with material from a national intelligence estimate, extend the projection beyond the NIE's normal five-year limit, and then add some evaluation by the policy-planners themselves. A second part may state alternative courses of action or what must be done in the situation. A third and final section is likely to make a series of recommendations in a rather discursive presentation. (If you want certain results, you will have to do these types of things.) Papers to be thrown into the National Security Council hopper are more apt to follow the special style developed for NSC papers.[4] NSC country policy papers, which are usually the responsibility of the Department of State (and of which over thirty exist), are drafted in five parts, the first of which includes an estimate of the political, economic, and military situation in the country studied, with a summary of its foreign policy and of its relations with the United States. A second section defines the degree of American interest in the country. How important is it politically and economically in a cold war context? What would be the effect if it moved further from the United States or were lost to the free world? A third section spells out American short-term and long-term objectives; a fourth describes what the United States can possibly do to further its interests and objectives in the existing situation; a fifth outlines alternative policies which may be followed if the situation changes radically or if it continues to develop along present lines.

The NSC paper is "kicked around" the Department for review

[4] Although the Policy Planning Staff did draft certain basic papers as the National Security Council policy structure was evolving, it does not undertake the direct drafting or revision of NSC country papers. A member of the Staff is usually present at policy discussions of such papers. The Policy Planning Staff would intervene to review such an NSC paper before it went to the NSC Planning Board only in an unusual and crucial situation. Coordination of preparation or revision of such NSC or OCB papers is now the responsibility of the regional bureaus.

and clearance (with a Policy Planning Staff member kibitzing in any policy conferences on the paper) until a Department position has been firmed up, but it is not presented to other agencies of the government until it comes up for discussion in a meeting of the NSC Planning Board Assistants. One member of the Policy Planning Staff is the regular representative of the Department at meetings of the NSC Board Assistants. The Board Assistants take the policy paper back to their agencies for consideration and brief the members of the NSC Planning Board which will meet for a preliminary discussion of the paper. State is represented on the NSC Planning Board by the Assistant Secretary for Policy Planning.

A member of the National Security Council Special Staff, assigned to the paper throughout its flow through the NSC machinery, considers the paper and briefs the NSC's representative to the NSC Planning Board (the Special Assistant to the President for National Security Affairs) who chairs meetings of the Board. At the Planning Board meeting, the agency differences are pointed up and the paper is returned to the Board Assistants for redrafting and resubmission. The suggestions of other agencies must be scrutinized by the Policy Planning Staff and operating officers in the Department directly concerned. On the basis of a new Department position, the assigned member of the Policy Planning Staff meets with the Board Assistants to negotiate a new draft of the paper.

The new draft is circulated, comments collected, a new position set for the Department, and the policy-planner on the Board Assistants briefs the Assistant Secretary for Policy Planning for the next round of Planning Board discussion. The NSC Planning Board's function is to prepare the policy paper in the best possible form, without concealing or glossing over department differences, for the consideration of the National Security Council. The paper may come before the Board on several occasions before being approved and forwarded to the NSC.

The approved version must be carefully studied at appropriate levels and areas in the Department, comments made, and the De-

partment's position agreed upon once again. Then the Assistant
Secretary for Policy Planning briefs the Secretary of State, the
Department's representative on the National Security Council.
The Special Assistant to the President for National Security Affairs
briefs the President of the United States, who normally presides
at NSC meetings. The Policy Planning Staff's responsibility ceases
only when the policy paper is finally approved by the President
after discussion before the National Security Council.

Reflecting upon the complexity of the process of channeling a
single NSC paper involving the Policy Planning Staff through the
ups and downs, reviewing and redrafting, until final acceptance by
the President, it is not surprising that members of the Policy Planning Staff sometimes feel that their participation in policy-making
—even at this level and on an advisory basis—limits to some degree the breadth of the long hard look into the future for which
the Policy Planning Staff was originally created.

Recent Policy Planning Staff operations in NSC channels have
not encouraged sweeping intellectual considerations or broad-
scale controversy. Many policy papers on country or functional
problems had been run through the NSC mill over the past twelve
years. When the papers have returned to the NSC and the Department for review, revision of detail was more likely than
complete reconstruction. Practical consistency required confining
thinking to a developing pattern. The increasing emphasis upon
refinement in detail narrowed the opportunities of the policy-
planners to plow new ground. Entranced with the present and
its smaller problems, the future stole on them unaware. The ar-
rival of the space age was unheralded. The grand reassessment
necessary to meet its new demands had not (and has not) been
carried out.

INFLUENCE

In setting up the Policy Planning Staff, Secretary of State
Marshall asked for a staff of "highly qualified thinkers," said they
were not to be "deluged with small stuff," gave them a conference
room adjoining his office, and tossed the problem of European recovery in their laps.

He got his "highly qualified thinkers." Of the original staff, Kennan is now with the Institute for Advanced Study at Princeton University, has produced excellent research studies and contributed influential analyses of contemporary events; Joseph Johnston is President of the Carnegie Endowment for International Peace. Working within the Department until recently was Jacques Reinstein as Director of the Office of German Affairs, who participated in the Foreign Service Institute's Senior Officer Course before reassignment. Ware Adams, now retired, served as Director of the Office of United Nations Political and Security Affairs until 1958. Carlton Savage remains with the Policy Planning Staff as its Executive Secretary.

Through the years there has been a parade of highly qualified personnel. They have wrestled with every major problem confronting American foreign policy in the post-World War II era; The Marshall Plan, NATO, Point Four, the Berlin Airlift, Korea (they foresaw the possibility of this event three months ahead), SEATO, the first Summit Conference, peaceful uses of atomic energy, Suez, the Hungarian revolt, the second Summit Conference and the German problem of 1959.

None of these questions was "small stuff," but not all came before the Staff for unhurried contemplation before action. Some were crisis situations in which American reaction might have long-range results, favorable or unfavorable to attainment of the nation's goals. It is unthinkable that the Staff should not be consulted for its advice in such instances, but with limited numbers the imposition of crash programs upon the Staff agenda detracts from the ability of its members to look ahead. It does keep them in touch with operational reality, however.

Secretary of State Dean Acheson used the Policy Planning Staff members as personal consultants and enjoyed participating in their free-wheeling discussions of world affairs. Kennan as Director of the Staff was the master chairman, drawing out differing points of view, summarizing the points of basic consensus, and leading the Staff toward an agreed policy position. As the Policy Planning Staff proved its usefulness, its operations were pinned down by additional responsibilities which lessened its freedom of action.

During the tenure of Nitze as Director of the Staff, Secretary Acheson called for advice from the Staff to operating bureaus on problems which might arise in three to six months, told it to keep current foreign policy under constant review and criticism, and finally sought quarterly projections of problems which might arise within a year.

Under the regime of Secretary of State Dulles, there were remarkable changes in relationships, responsibilities, and methods of operation of the Policy Planning Staff. Some saw these changes as representing a downgrading of the Staff's position and influence. Others viewed the changes as necessary in the light of developing conditions, as maintaining or even enhancing the influence of the Staff.

Political scientists sometimes measure importance and prestige in government by certain symbols—the size of desks, whether walls are painted or panelled, and type of floor covering (the thickest carpets or none at all). Additional factors observed are changes in physical location of a functionary's office or staff, in his title, or in the places where he appears in the conduct of his duties. These are often legitimate tools of analysis, but they must be used with discretion.

As the workload of the Secretary of State increased, the direct relationship of the Policy Planning Staff to the Secretary tended to diminish. It finally lost its conference room adjoining Secretary Dulles' office to the Assistant Secretary of State for Public Affairs; its conference room and offices are now physically more closely related to the office of the Under Secretary. This move, while significant as a temporary upgrading of the public information function, did not necessarily imply any net loss of influence by the Policy Planning Staff. Secretary Dulles had never consulted with the Staff as a whole, preferring to deal with it through its Director.

Following this physical change, the Director was also named Assistant Secretary of State for Policy Planning. This appeared to be a promotion, since in the title structure the heads of offices in a bureau are directors while the bureau chiefs are generally Assistant Secretaries. But it is likely that an Assistant Secretary is less closely attached to the Secretary of State than, let us say, the Director of the Executive Secretariat. The additional title for its Director tended to move the Policy Planning Staff from a position as a close personal staff attached to the Office of the Secretary to one among a number of competing areas and bureaus. Even this is inconclusive as a measure of the influence of the Policy Planning Staff.

If the position of the Staff as a whole in relationship to the Secretary appears to have deteriorated, it may be pointed out that Assistant Secretary Bowie and later Assistant Secretary Smith accompanied Secretary Dulles to many international conferences, undoubtedly having opportunities to bring the thinking of policy-planners to bear in crucial negotiations conducted by the Secretary.

More important in altering the position of the Policy Planning Staff in its degree of influence upon policy-making was the rise of the National Security Council as a government-wide structure. This not only affected the Policy Planning Staff but placed the Department of State in a new role as well.

The Policy Planning Staff got off to a fast start with its study of European economic recovery and the fact that it was created two and a half months before the National Security Council was approved by Public Law 253 of the Eightieth Congress on July 26, 1947. The broader and more intricate NSC machinery was clumsy and ponderous compared to the high-powered intellectual thrust of the tightly-knit Planning Staff. The historic primacy of the Department of State in foreign affairs buttressed the influence of the policy-planners and tended to inhibit development of the National Security Council as chief adviser to the President on national security affairs—including foreign policy.

During the first Eisenhower administration, the National Security Council gathered momentum and finally emerged as the dominant factor. The Policy Planning Staff and the Department of State were now one step removed from the President in their role as advisers on foreign policy. Because of the President's high personal regard for Secretary Dulles, the significance of the change did not immediately become fully apparent. The Department of

State still stood a little more equal than others in NSC negotiations, although on occasion it was overruled.

The relationship of the Policy Planning Staff to the National Security Council structure is clearly subordinate, but the channels provided by the NSC machinery for transmitting the ideas of the policy planners to other agencies of government have in a sense broadened the Staff's impact upon the policy-making process. It may be unfair to say that the influence of the Policy Planning Staff is less than in its formative years, but one must admit that it is different.

In the early days, the Policy Planning Staff was completely outside policy-making channels. Its influence on the operators and decision-makers was a question of salesmanship of good ideas. Members of the Staff had to go to bat for Policy Planning decisions and convince the operators to back up their recommendations or advice to the Secretary. This need has not been completely obviated, but participation in the formulation and revision of NSC policies gives the Staff regularized and routine means of influencing Department opinion (through kibitzing on policy discussions in the operating bureaus). Consultation with Department operating officers is a two-way selling device, but the Staff's developing relationship with the NSC complex has given it some leverage in dealing with the operating level. It is difficult to by-pass on NSC questions.

Gerard C. Smith, appointed in 1958 as the fourth Director of the Staff, with becoming modesty and considerable accuracy once said: "We do not on the Staff purport to do any master planning of foreign policy." Nonetheless, the Policy Planning Staff as the chief backstop of the Secretary in the National Security Council proceedings, with representation on the Planning Board and the Board Assistants, certainly affects and exerts influence upon Department of State positions and NSC policies.

CONCLUSIONS

The Policy Planning Staff's functions are carried out both externally, in relationship to the National Security Council, and internally, within the Department. If it tries to keep its eyes on the road ahead, there are times when it must devote its attention to the crisis which is immediately at hand. The illusion that a highly capable Staff with its specifically assigned functions can, like Nero, fiddle while Rome burns has been dispelled by the overwhelming complexities confronting the policy-makers in our day. In meeting policy problems of whatever type, the Policy Planning Staff contributes a perspective of place and time, blending and building consistency in policies for wide areas, trying to make certain that we apply our resources to meet at least the immediate future rather than the past.

The effectiveness of the Policy Planning Staff depends upon the quality of its director and personnel and upon its relationships to the Secretary of State.

Even more, its performance may depend upon the leadership and courage of the President in the National Security Council, and upon whether he recognizes when to call for fundamental reassessment of the assumptions upon which all NSC policies are built.

Men can be great only in great times. The Policy Planning Staff will draw the best from its personnel only when the President and the Secretary of State confront it with seemingly unsolvable and overwhelming problems. If American foreign policy is content to wage peace in our time, without searching diligently for the means of alleviating basic causes of international tension, the policy planners will perform adequately but without great distinction.

There is little doubt that the Staff will continue to perform a planning function important to the conduct of our foreign relations. Whether, in addition, the Policy Planning Staff contributes to the development of a brave new world—in which the United States continues to play a secure and prosperous part—seems likely to depend upon Presidents and Secretaries of State yet to come.

Part Three

PUBLIC OPINION

5 Legislative Liaison Specialists
Two-Way Conduit

FUNCTIONS

If the checks and balances written into the Constitution by the founding fathers are an open invitation for conflict between our executive and legislative branches of government, the role of the legislative liaison staff in the Congressional Relations Area of the Department of State is—at very least—to civilize the struggle by fostering accommodation between contending parties on matters affecting foreign policy.

The job of the Congressional Relations Area of the Department of State is to interpret Congress to the Department, and the Department to Congress. As its Assistant Secretary, his Deputy, and the legislative liaison specialists shuttle back and forth down Constitution and Independence Avenues they serve as a two-way conduit between Capitol Hill and Foggy Bottom.[1] They pick up ideas rather than pollen, but their movements across town provide for a cross-fertilization as productive as a bee's flight. Without the Area and its staff functioning as a channel of communication and coordination between the executive and legislative branches of government, the fruitful implementation of a legislative program and a general foreign policy with effective public support would be more difficult to achieve.

As one Assistant Secretary of State for Congressional Relations has explained, the Area staff actually performs four functions, two of which are internal; two, external. Within the executive branch of government, it helps to formulate the Administration's foreign

[1] "Foggy Bottom" is derived from the Department's location near the Potomac River and is a term often used by journalists, sometimes to denote a real or imagined lack of foresight by policy-makers in the Department.

affairs legislative program. In carrying out this function, it cooperates with bureaus and areas of the Department, with other departments and agencies, and with the Bureau of the Budget in the Executive Office of the President.

Also, within the executive branch, the staff members participate in policy conferences, contributing to the formulation of non-legislative policy decisions important enough to be of general interest to members of Congress. In performing both internal functions, the Congressional Relations Area is in part the representative of the legislative interest, in part the adviser on how Department interests can be accommodated with congressional views. There are times, certainly, when the congressional factor is weighed less heavily than other considerations by Department decision-makers (and one can sometimes be thankful for their courage at these moments), but even in this situation they have been made to understand and consider the congressional position (even though they believed their own decision was more in the national interest).

In its external relations with Congress, the Area staff serves as a funnel into the Department for congressional requests which are sent to experts for reply, and serves as a funnel out of the Department for information to members of Congress and their constituents concerning either legislative or non-legislative questions related to the Department or foreign policy.

Also, in its external relations with Congress, the staff of the Area consults with, and encourages Department leaders to consult with, members of Congress on foreign policy questions.

ORGANIZATION AND PERSONNEL

The Assistant Secretary for Congressional Relations heads one of the smallest staffs ever placed under an Assistant Secretary in the Department of State. To have it otherwise might place the legislative liaison program in serious jeopardy. Congress traditionally has taken a dim view of large congressional relations staffs in government departments and agencies. The average member of the House or Senate undoubtedly feels that there are enough private lobbyists infesting the corridors on Capitol Hill without spending tax funds to create a bevy of public counterparts. Naturally, Congress does not want to increase its problem of competing with the executive branch in the field of foreign policy by appropriating public monies with which the Department could possibly exert undue influence over congressional voting patterns.

The Congressional Relations Area in the Department is modest enough in size, with only twenty-three employees, over half of whom are performing secretarial duties. Below the level of Assistant and Deputy Assistant Secretary, tenure has tended to be permanent (even though most of the legislative liaison specialists serve in exempt or Schedule C positions [2]). One Deputy Assistant Secretary and one legislative liaison specialist took advantage of Wristonization to enter the Foreign Service and gave up their positions in the Congressional Relations Area.

Traditionally, the Assistant Secretary spends most of his time "on the Hill" conducting the external relations of the Area. The Deputy Assistant Secretary devotes himself more to administration and the internal relations between the Area and the Department itself, although he also may appear at hearings and talk with members of Congress informally in their offices. A Deputy Assistant Secretary for Mutual Security Affairs was created in 1958 when the Department took over from the International Cooperation Administration responsibility for preparation and presentation of mutual security legislation to the Congress. The new post is manned by a former legislative liaison specialist who has had long experience with atomic energy and mutual security questions.

Three men and one woman serve as legislative management liaison specialists. One of the specialists works internally with the Bureaus of European, Near Eastern and South Asian, and Economic Affairs; externally with such congressional committees as Foreign Relations and Foreign Affairs, Interstate and Foreign Commerce, Ways and Means, Banking and Currency, and Agriculture. A second specialist concentrates internally on the Bureaus of Far Eastern and International Organization Affairs (and on problems concerning fisheries and wildlife). This specialist also

---

[2] Schedule C positions are those which may be filled by appointments from outside the Civil Service or Foreign Service.

works with the Foreign Relations and Foreign Affairs Committees, the Interstate and Foreign Commerce Committees, and the House Merchant Marine and Fisheries Committee. A third legislative liaison specialist concentrates within the Department on relations with the Bureaus of African Affairs, Security and Consular Affairs,[3] Administration, Intelligence and Research, and the Office of the Legal Adviser. In Congress, this specialist works with the Judiciary Committees and with the Foreign Relations and Foreign Affairs Committees. A fourth specialist (the lone Foreign Service officer serving in the Congressional Relations Area) concentrates on the Bureaus of Inter-American Affairs and Public Affairs within the Department (as well as questions concerning atomic energy, disarmament, and the Foreign Service), maintains external relations with the Foreign Relations and Foreign Affairs Committees, the Post Office and Civil Service Committees, and the Joint Committee on Atomic Energy.

A legislative reports section and a non-legislative requests section complete the major elements in the organization of the Congressional Relations Area. Coordination of staffwork in the Area is furthered by staff meetings each morning at 8:45. The Assistant Secretary attends the Secretary of State's daily briefing and staff conference at 9:15 A.M. Thus, he can serve as a channel up to the Secretary from his staff, and as a channel down from the Secretary.

CHANGING NEEDS AND NEW PROBLEMS

The maintenance of an agreeable working relationship with Congress has been a Department interest of long standing. It is significant, however, that no top-level Department official was assigned legislative liaison as his *only* responsibility until 1949.[4] That this step would become inevitable could have been forecast

---

[3] The Bureau of Consular and Security Affairs is responsible for passports and visas, as well as certain other consular activities. Among its duties is the responsibility for security clearance of personnel with access to classified documents, and such other ill-assorted assignments as "munitions control" and "refugee and migration affairs."

[4] Although few Department personnel associated with the Congressional Relations Area are now aware of it, there is one exception to this blanket statement.

at the conclusion of "the fifteen weeks," that dramatic period between February 21 and June 5, 1947, when United States policy-makers came squarely to grips with destiny and committed the nation to responsible leadership in world affairs.[5] This assumption of a positive role, not from desire but from a realization that economic and political chaos might destroy freedom and democracy in the Western world, required congressional support, thrust matters of foreign policy uppermost in the minds of Senators and Representatives (if not in those of many of their constituents).

For a brief time, before the depth and permanence of the American commitment was fully understood, the Assistant Secretaries and other high-level officials of the Department were drawn into congressional liaison almost daily on an *ad hoc* basis, whenever the need arose to explain legislative measures or general foreign policy to members of Congress. As valuable as this experience was in a transition period, both to Congressmen and Department officers, the time involved seriously impaired the ability of Department leaders to perform properly their policy-making functions. The amount of consultation and briefing desirable from day to day was too large to be absorbed in its entirety by action officers.

The creation of a full-time Assistant Secretary for Congressional Relations, with a small staff of about twenty (including clerical personnel), was a most modest adjustment of Department organization to routinize the process of explaining and justifying the multiple facets of an evolving foreign policy to members of Congress. As Congress responded to world conditions and began legislative consideration of foreign economic assistance and defensive alliances, the responsibility of the Congressional Relations Area to brief action officers and policy-planners in the Department on the

---

Dean Acheson, as Assistant Secretary for Congressional Relations from May 1945 until August 1945 before he became Under Secretary, had no other responsibility. Few now recall that responsibility for International Conferences was separated from the Congressional Relations post as Acheson moved into the position for a brief period. Following Acheson's elevation to Under Secretary, the title of Assistant Secretary for Congressional Relations lapsed until the appointment of Ernest Gross to the post early in 1949.

[5] Joseph M. Jones, *The Fifteen Weeks,* New York: The Viking Press, 1955.

status of legislation on Capitol Hill, and to coordinate the appearance of Department officials at legislative hearings, became increasingly important.

The historic primacy of the Committee on Foreign Relations of the Senate and the Committee on Foreign Affairs of the House in the field of foreign policy, coupled with the influence of committee chairmen like the late Senator Arthur Vandenberg, for a time made it possible for the Department to concentrate its major attention upon relatively small leadership groups, who in turn could project an understanding and acceptance of Administration measures among a majority of the members of Congress.

As foreign policy moved toward the center of the stage in congressional affairs, dealing with an ever-widening variety of topics and promising political prominence to the ambitious and able who could exert effective influence upon the end products approved by Congress, other committees—either by right or by aspiration—challenged the exclusive leadership of the Foreign Relations and Foreign Affairs Committees. A dispersion of power both among and within congressional committees, hastened by the seniority rule for selection of committee chairmen, which on occasion elevated the aged or infirm to leadership of the Foreign Relations or Foreign Affairs Committees, complicated the legislative liaison function of the Department of State. (The vigor of Senator William Fulbright, who became chairman of the still powerful Senate Foreign Relations Committee at age fifty-three, may retard decentralization, but even he may find the process difficult to reverse.)

Working with approximately the same number of liaison personnel, confronted by a multiplying number of committee leaders (each of whom was important in certain specific aspects of foreign policy but few of whom could command wide followership in the Senate or House), the Congressional Relations Area was forced by circumstances to raise its sights; it had to attempt to work increasingly through the leadership of the Senate and House, with men like Lyndon Johnson, Everett Dirksen, Sam Rayburn and Charles Halleck. (Not that it has always done this, but it is slowly learning. Johnson and Rayburn were almost completely ignored on foreign policy matters during the first Eisenhower administration.)

Dealing with leaders of an opposition party, as well as political leaders representing the Administration, and with an increasing number of committee chairmen, only some of whom have had a long interest in foreign policy and possess a degree of expertise which might lead them at times to subordinate political considerations, poses a new and critical problem in the performance of the congressional liaison function. These conditions may require a willingness for consultation, a spirit of bipartisanship, and qualities of statesmanship which strain the diplomatic capacities of the mere mortals who serve at high levels in Congress and the Department. President Eisenhower and Premier Nikita Khrushchev sometimes appeared little farther apart than former Secretary Dulles and Senator Fulbright on questions of foreign policy.

The necessity of legislative liaison with congressional leaders and committee chairmen does not allow the legislative relations specialists of the Department to ignore any of the 100 Senators or 437 Representatives—(or members of their staffs, who themselves play an important role in influencing the decisions of their legislative employers). Even just plain Congressmen consider themselves as equals with their leaders ("We're all elected by the people."), although recognizing that some among their number are more equal than others.

If one grants the importance of the proper organization and performance of the legislative liaison function in the rocket age and is concerned by the problems which confront the Congressional Relations Area in carrying out its assigned responsibilities, a more detailed look at the work of the Area and its liaison specialists is necessary.

LEGISLATIVE MANAGEMENT AND LIAISON

Central staff figures in the conduct of the Department's relations with Congress are the Area's four legislative management specialists. (The term "management" implies an oversight responsibility for planning of the Department's legislative program internally and by no stretch of the imagination suggests any power to manage members of Congress themselves.) The terminology stems from the day not long ago when two of the four functioned from their offices in the Department, often in contact by telephone with committee staff members or Congressmen but not engaging in face-to-face liaison. Two of the four were liaison officers, did leg work on the Hill; one maintained relations with the Senate; the other, with the House.

In 1957 responsibilities were reorganized. All four specialists began to divide their time between the Department and Capitol Hill. Voices became persons; relations were humanized. The increase in direct exchange was of value to the Department and to Congress. Today, the officers are both legislative management and legislative liaison specialists. The latter term becomes the more diplomatic and is less easily misunderstood.

Many members of congressional committees with foreign affairs responsibilities, either directly or through their staff assistants, contact the Department liaison specialists on their own initiative. Others have been less aware of the services provided by the specialists. Letters and personal calls to offices on the Hill are slowly establishing broader relationships. One problem is the workload, of both the specialists and members of Congress, which largely limits personal exchanges to Saturdays.

Much of the time of the liaison specialists is taken up with internal functions. They participate actively in policy conferences if legislative implementation will be required or if the policy may have congressional repercussions. They may sit in at increasingly higher levels of consideration of such policy, even meeting with the Under Secretary or Secretary, although the Assistant Secretary for Congressional Relations or his Deputy would be more likely to take over as the question reaches top policy-making officers.

Their role in policy conferences is to give advice on what congressional reaction will be on the alternative proposals under consideration. They suggest how a policy should be presented to muster the greatest support, advising on form, substance, and strategy. Almost everyone in the Department considers himself an expert on Congress, so the job of the liaison specialist is no bed of roses; he must prove his points.

Most complex and prolonged of the annual responsibilities of the legislative liaison specialists is that of assisting the Assistant Secretary for Congressional Relations in the coordination and implementation of the Department's legislative program. Early each fall, while most members of Congress are touring the hustings to sample sentiment at the grass roots, Department officers are asked to draw up statements concerning all questions pertaining to their areas or functions which may later require legislative action.

Items are included which may be only a gleam in the initiator's eye as well as those which are certain to demand a place in the legislative program to be submitted by the Administration during the next session of Congress. This broad and rather unselective list is submitted by the Department to the Bureau of the Budget in the Executive Office of the President. It is circulated by the Bureau of the Budget to other departments and agencies in the government for comment. Proposals from other Departments related to questions of foreign policy are forwarded by the Bureau to the Department of State for comment. This launching of a series of trial balloons, with critical departmental analysis puncturing those which are unlikely to receive general support within the executive branch, indicates to the Department of State the legislative areas in which it can proceed with some hope of success.

Normally, not more than half a dozen major legislative matters are given priority and high-lighted in the Department's legislative planning, which now goes into high gear. For example, major items in the Department's legislative program for 1957 were the Eisenhower Doctrine for the Middle East, the Mutual Security Program, the Atomic Energy Agency Statute, and the authorization of American membership in the Organization for Trade Co-operation. The Department batted .750 that year, for only OTC failed to receive congressional approval.

A series of secondary measures are also pushed, but many of these are somewhat routine matters, like double-taxation agreements or treaties of friendship, commerce, and navigation. The secondary measures, upon which an agreed executive branch policy can be speedily achieved, may be cleared and forwarded to committee staffs by October. It is wise to have them ready for committee action early in the session, before partisan passions are aroused, and before hearings on controversial issues demand so much time that matters of lesser importance are pushed aside, although they require only perfunctory consideration.

Even measures which are controversial must be ready as early as possible, so that the Congress will have sufficient time to engage in rather prolonged hearings. If they are reported out of committee too near the end of a session, the measures will not receive adequate debate on the floor or compete successfully for the attention of the broad membership in the cloakrooms just off the chambers of the House and Senate.

Inter-departmental policy formulation through the National Security Council structure and agreements for implementation arrived at by Operations Coordinating Board procedures may have led to the particular legislative measure which must now run the department and inter-departmental legislative gantlet, before final clearance by the Bureau of the Budget and consideration by Congress.

Any legislative matter of primary concern to the Department but clearly of inter-departmental interest will have to work up through the Department—sometimes subject to review at all levels from the regional or functional desk to the Secretary—in a search for internal accommodation and agreement. Inter-departmental committees will then meet, with a staff member from the Bureau of the Budget keeping a watchful eye over developments, to beat out an agreed Administration position and policy.

The products of this consideration are forwarded to the Bureau of the Budget and circulated to the interested departments for final clearance. If critical comments are still returned, the Bureau of the Budget casts the problem back to the departments for further discussion, and a higher-level inter-agency committee wrestles with the differences which have come to light. (These latter conferences may be at the Assistant Secretary or Deputy Under Secretary level.)

This process of negotiation-reconsideration could go on endlessly, without accord being reached. If the matter is one which the President considers of sufficient importance, it may be forwarded to him via the Bureau of the Budget through an Assistant (like Eisenhower's Wilton B. Persons). The President makes a decision; his staff raps departmental knuckles; and all the departments fall in line. Knowledge that the head-knocking process is held in reserve forces accommodation short of the summit on most matters, all except those involving the most fundamental differences of opinion between the departments.

The legislative liaison specialists have followed these processes from the very beginning, keeping the heat on Department officers from the original draft, through Department clearance and interagency clearance, to approval by the Bureau of the Budget and inclusion of the measure as part of the President's legislative program.

Now their attention shifts to the planning of Department and other appearances on the Hill in support of any measures for which the Department of State is assigned primary legislative responsibility by the Bureau of the Budget. The Congressional Relations Area actually has the authority delegated by the Secretary to determine who shall testify from within the Department in behalf of measures, and can work directly or through the Bureau of the Budget to line up supporting testimony from other agencies.

A major problem is protecting the Secretary from having to appear at hearings on every piece of legislation. All committees are interested in having him testify, either for major Department measures or on those where State's interest is secondary and which are being pressed by another department. Assistant Secretaries and Office Directors appear as the Department's principal witnesses on many items. At executive sessions of committees, even country or functional experts of desk level and legislative liaison specialists give valuable testimony.

Through cooperation with organization liaison officers in the

Department's Office of Public Services, it is sometimes possible to arrange for national organizations with an interest in foreign policy legislation to be alerted so that they may appear if they desire at committee hearings in support of the Department's program.

Although no legislative liaison specialist would say that any congressional committee or its staff was anything but friendly, it is obvious to the average housewife who irons while she watches hearings on TV, or to the professor who observes committee proceedings in person, that even in public some committees are more friendly than others. Generally speaking, committees with the longest experience in dealing with the Department are the most cooperative, realizing that to get the information they want as quickly as possible will require adequate preparation of Department personnel who testify before them.

Committee staff members and liaison specialists work cooperatively to arrange when hearings will be held, depending on when the committee can work hearings into its crowded schedule, and when the Department's principal witnesses can be ready to appear and won't be shuttling between Paris and Manila. They exchange information on a daily basis by telephone.

Since committee staffs are often responsible for drafting some of the questions which may be posed to those appearing at hearings, they are at times in a position to give the Department a rough idea of the factors which disturb the Committee well in advance of the hearing. If it appears that questioning may be dominated by members of the committee opposed to the legislation, it is sometimes possible to work cooperatively with the committee staff to formulate questions which will allow a balanced exploration of all sides of the point at issue.

Briefing the Secretary of State for his appearances before congressional committees varies, depending upon the Secretary's knowledge of the topic. A Secretary like John Foster Dulles, more interested in politico-legal affairs than those of an economic nature, would be given extensive briefings before appearing on economic measures, such as trade agreements. The Assistant Secretary for Economic Affairs, who does much of the Department's testifying on the Hill in behalf of economic legislation, was in charge of a two-hour briefing for Secretary Dulles in 1957 when the late Secretary appeared in behalf of legislation to authorize United States participation in the Organization for Trade Cooperation.

Before the oral briefing, the area and functional bureaus of the Department primarily interested in the subject matter (in behalf of which the Secretary is to testify) will draft and clear thorough briefing books which the Secretary will study prior to his appearance before the committee. For example, the 1957 briefing book on legislation to authorize American membership in the Organization for Trade Cooperation was more than a hundred pages in length, included a twenty-two-page opening statement for the Secretary to make to the committee. In addition, the book contained a series of questions on the text of the OTC charter, with answers explaining various parts of the text in some detail; a similar series of questions on the General Agreement on Tariffs and Trade; a comparison between the charter of OTC and that of the International Trade Organization; a discussion of legal and Constitutional questions involved; and a series of statements and documents which had been issued by other government agencies on the OTC.

The Secretary is so well prepared (although, because of the time factor, never quite as well as the staff would like him to be) when he appears to testify that after his introductory statement he is likely to answer questions without referring to the briefing book.

Representatives of the Congressional Relations Area are present at all hearings involving Department of State legislation, and will also be in the galleries or corridors during debate of legislation on the Senate or House floor. As the debate rages on the floor, the Assistant Secretary for Congressional Relations (and the legislative liaison specialists) may hold tense, hurried conferences with floor managers and administration leaders to determine whether the measure should be voted on as it stands or whether the Department can accept changes to gain more wide-spread support without damaging the measure's effectiveness irreparably.

Indeed, the legislative liaison specialist follows the piece of legislation from its inception to its passage or demise, guiding, advising, explaining, even compromising, until its fate is finally determined. He may have to return to the Department at the end of this vigil bearing a lifeless legislative measure which he puts in the files until new life can be breathed into it come another year or another Congress.

Legislative Requests and Reports

Any major government agency with the wide range of legislative interests and contacts of the Department of State finds it necessary to centralize the multiplicity of rather routine tasks which assist in keeping policy-making officials informed of congressional action. In addition, there must obviously be a central check-point on congressional requests and Department answers on legislative questions. Two persons in the Congressional Relations Area perform these functions.

Each morning when they arrive for work at 8:45 A.M., they find on their desks copies of yesterday's *Congressional Record*, delivered by Department messengers from the Government Printing Office. By 11 A.M., the two legislative reporters have prepared a two- to three-page summary which is forwarded to the Policy and Reports Staff of the Executive Secretariat for distribution to top-level officers in the Department. This summary presents four types of information on each branch of Congress: (1) Whether or not it is meeting and what it is scheduled to take up, (2) committees which will meet and the topics upon which they are holding hearings, (3) a resumé of yesterday's proceedings, and (4) bills and resolutions introduced, passed, or progressing from one stage of consideration to another.

Between 11 A.M., and 2 P.M., the reporters prepare a so-called *Daily Summary*, eight to twelve pages long, which is issued for distribution with the Executive Secretariat's *Secret Summary* at

3 P.M., to key Department officers. It is a detailed listing under topic headings of bills, reports, and speeches bearing on foreign policy, with the pages on which the reference appears, in the *Congressional Record* of the preceding day. The *Daily Summary* is also forwarded to many other agencies, including the International Cooperation Administration, the United States Information Agency, the Senate Committee on Foreign Relations, the House Committee on Foreign Affairs, and the Library of Congress. About 600 copies are mimeographed for internal and external use.

In addition to the *Record*, every bill, hearing, report, resolution, or act of the House and Senate is forwarded to the two reporters. They must go through this mass of material and select those documents which have a relation to the Department, either on administrative or substantive issues. One copy is filed (their file is complete from 1944). A second copy is sent to the legislative liaison specialist dealing with this type of legislation; a third, forwarded to the area or bureau in the Department most concerned.

All requests for information addressed to the Department on questions of legislation, whether they come from members of Congress, from congressional committees, or from the Bureau of the Budget, are channeled across the desks of the two reporters. They handled 880 requests concerning legislation during the Eighty-fourth Congress, first session, and 957 requests during the second session. An officer in the Department is assigned to draft a reply; the reporters try to expedite action on the request if the answer is delayed. They check on Department clearances, make sure it is routed to the Bureau of the Budget for clearance, forward the report for signature as finally approved to the Assistant Secretary for Congressional Relations, and then make certain the report is dispatched to the Congressman or committee which requested it. Their file of such reports, which represents the view and comments of the Department on legislation, is complete from 1944.

On a weekly basis, the reporters issue a document called "Legislation and Legislative Reports Cleared through H." (In view of the complexity of the processes just described, it should be pointed out that "H" stands for Congressional Relations Area.) This document lists any report which has entered or left the Department, to either Congress or the Bureau of the Budget, with the date it cleared their office. This summary lists Department clearances and enables an officer who has been unintentionally or intentionally omitted to catch up with the paper, if it hasn't been finally dispatched from the Department, and to check it for clearance.

NON-LEGISLATIVE REQUESTS AND CONGRESSIONAL MAIL

Congressmen make greater use of the Department of State for information on foreign policy questions than they do of the Foreign Affairs Division of their own Legislative Reference Service in the Library of Congress (which handles over 4,000 requests per year). One legislative officer in the Congressional Relations Area serves as a check-point on telephone calls and mail from members of Congress and their staffs requesting non-legislative information concerning policy, operations, or administration of American foreign relations. It is a one-man operation, but with well over 5,000 telephone calls and approximately 6,000 letters to be expedited each year. Fortunately, the resources of the entire Department are at his disposal.

Telephone calls pour in at the rate of twenty to forty per day. An aide calls to gather material for a Senator who is giving a speech on the Foreign Service. A Congressman calls on behalf of a constituent who wishes to shoot buffalo in India; can he? If so, where? Someone wants to have an accurate list of the times the United Nations has acted on the question of admitting Communist China. A congressional staffer calls in behalf of a constituent back home in the district who wants to practice law before consular courts (which, it turns out, no longer exist).

The legislative officer scribbles the requests down on a sheet of legal-size yellow lined paper, with perhaps four or five lines of information on each query. With two phones in use simultaneously a good bit of the time, he takes a request on one phone and while the caller waits gets in touch with the person who has the answer on the other, then relays the information back over the first phone.

If the request is more complicated, he may transfer the call to a Department expert, then call back later to make sure that the person making the request got the information desired. If filling the request requires several days, he will keep the matter under surveillance until the request has been answered. There can be few slip-ups or Congressmen will wonder about the Department's efficiency.

All congressional mail is microfilmed when it comes into the Department. Analysts assign it to the proper regional or functional bureau (or area) for action. If the letter is "hot" enough, it goes directly to the Assistant Secretary for Congressional Relations for quick handling at top levels and is microfilmed later. Letters forwarded by Congressmen for constituents are often referred to Public Correspondence in the Office of Public Services in the Bureau of Public Affairs, particularly if the problems raised are broad ones on which the Department needs to formulate a general policy statement for public distribution.

All Congressional mail is given top priority and is supposed to clear the Department within three days. The legislative officer has an index card on each piece of mail which lists the time it arrived in the Department and who is the action officer. As the deadline nears, he checks to see if it will be out on time. Most of the letters must be signed by the Assistant Secretary for Congressional Relations.

The process of clearance of a congressional letter is the same as that required for any policy statement released by the Department. All interested bureaus must give clearance before it may be forwarded to the member of Congress. On most letters this involves a check on the contents, probably drafted at the desk level, by two to four Office Directors or Deputy Assistant Secretaries in as many bureaus.

If the clearance process is held up by disagreement and the necessity to hold conferences to reach accommodation (or for any other reason) but it appears that an answer can be produced in several days, the legislative officer may call to explain the delay and inform the person making the request approximately when an answer will be forthcoming. If the delay will be even longer, a matter requiring inter-agency clearance, he drafts a letter acknowledging receipt of the request and notes when an answer can be expected.

As a letter clears the Department, signed by the Assistant Secretary, the legislative officer records Department clearances (and those with outside agencies) and the date on the index card. Letters do get lost in the dark recesses of the Department because they pass through so many hands, and there is always the possibility of human error. The fact that they rarely do go astray may be attributed in part to the eternal vigilance of the legislative officer.

LEADERSHIP AND DEVICES

Setting the tone of the Department's relations with the Congress at any given time, of course, is the Secretary of State. The Secretary's attitudes toward congressional relations are affected by his experiences before assuming office, actual relationships with Congress during his period of service, world conditions, and domestic political exigencies. His response and sensitivity to the need for congressional cooperation in the implementation of legislation or in support of general foreign policy will possibly be communicated to the President and color his relations with Congress, will certainly determine who will be selected to serve as Assistant Secretary of State for Congressional Relations, and will influence the choice or emphasis of special devices employed in maintaining liaison with Congress.

During the period since the permanent establishment of the Congressional Relations Area, there have been Assistant Secretaries of at least four types. The appointment of each type has its advantages (one may also assume, its disadvantages) and may be indicative of the current atmosphere of legislative-executive relations in the foreign policy field. There is the "substantive expert type," exemplified by Ernest Gross, who served in 1949 as the Assistant Secretary for Congressional Relations, and later rendered valuable service for the United States as a representative at the United

Nations; the "legislative professional staff type," represented by Jack McFall, who had long years of service on the staff of a congressional committee before his appointment as Assistant Secretary; "the congressional type," represented by Thruston Morton and Robert C. Hill, both of whom had served in the House of Representatives before appointment; and the "personal representative type," of which William B. Macomber, Jr., may be considered characteristic, with experience as a legislative assistant to a Senator but assuming his post as an Assistant Secretary after several years' service as a Special Assistant to the Secretary of State. There may be other types in the future, but these four were dominant during the past decade.

One may assume, without criticizing any of these five very able men, that their roles in relationship to Congress have been quite different. Gross was technically competent on substantive issues but no public relations man. His work on the Hill carried weight only because of his stature as an expert on foreign policy matters. His appointment was in keeping with the traditional conduct of Department relations with Congress. His successor was McFall, quite a different type of individual, particularly useful at a time when the Department was finding it necessary to experiment with new congressional liaison practices; because of McFall's staff experience, he was used to dealing deferentially yet influentially with members of Congress. He introduced or helped initiate a number of useful devices to bridge the gap between the Department and Congress, based on his appreciation of congressional attitudes.

The appointments of Morton and Hill indicated the more firm approach of an equal. By this time the Department's post-war policy programs and its liaison program were well established and had been reasonably successful, and the appointment of "members of the club" seemed the best way to deal "straight from the shoulder" with the House and Senate. Dependence on Congress (or subservience to it) during this period was less than it had been earlier.

The crises in the Middle East and Central Europe during the

fall of 1956 which precipitated difficulties in legislative-executive relations may have influenced adoption of the fourth approach, but in part the appointment of Macomber was dictated by the new need of the Secretary and the Department to deal directly with top leaders of Congress as a whole as well as with the lower-ranking and more dispersed leadership level represented by the committee chairmen.

Macomber, as Assistant Secretary for Congressional Relations, probably had more personal contacts with the Secretary than any other single Assistant Secretary in the Department. (During the Morton and Hill periods, it may be presumed that the Assistant Secretary for Public Affairs held this distinction.) He spoke personally for the Secretary every day on Capitol Hill as he talked with congressional leaders, committee chairmen, and members of influential committees. These men knew their ideas could be transmitted to the Secretary in person by the Assistant Secretary. He was the Secretary's voice, eyes, and ears on the Hill. This represents the most direct relationship a busy Secretary of State can maintain with Congress on a day-to-day basis if he is to fulfill his primary responsibilities as a decision-maker and Department leader.

Macomber was an innovator. To make new Senators aware of the Department and its procedures, he invited neophytes to breakfast early in February, 1959 to chat with the Secretary, the Under Secretary, the Under Secretary for Economic Affairs, the Deputy Under Secretaries, and the Assistant Secretaries. After breakfast, they attended the Secretary's morning staff conference, heard the regular intelligence briefing by the Director of Intelligence and Research, and listened to the discussion of operational problems among the Department's top officials. Later, new members of the House of Representatives, invited in three separate groups, were to enjoy the same opportunity and hospitality.

During the Lebanon Crisis of 1958, when American marines had been landed in the Near East, Assistant Secretary Macomber held twice-weekly discussions on Capitol Hill, each Tuesday and Thursday at 4 P.M., for members of the Senate Foreign Relations and

House Foreign Affairs Committees, or any other members of the Senate or House who cared to attend. Accompanied by a Department expert, he explained the most recent developments and helped answer questions.

Macomber breathed some life into the consultative subcommittees of the Senate Foreign Relations and House Foreign Affairs Committees by making it clear that briefing or discussion sessions of the subcommittees can be called by either the Department or the Congress. In the early days of the subcommittees, meetings were initiated by the Department. When the numbers of such sessions scheduled fell off between 1953 and 1956, some members of the Senate and House "did a slow burn." Senate consultations fell from twenty-nine in 1953 to six in 1956. A promising consultative device was in danger of withering on the vine. Macomber helped restore some of its vigor (although workloads in Congress and the Department limit the number of consultations).

McFall, too, was an initiator. He helped to plan the early briefing conferences held by the Department in 1951 for members of the House and Senate to give them a better idea of the new responsibilities confronting the United States in the post-World War II era. The evening "parties," paid for by sizable assessments upon the private funds of the Assistant Secretaries and other top Department officers, were a useful and ingenious device in mass education.

McFall encouraged Foreign Service officers in Washington for reassignment to visit the Congressmen from their home districts, to talk with them informally about their experiences and impressions overseas. This served as a means of humanizing and personalizing the Foreign Service at a time when considerable misapprehension existed among members of Congress concerning the ability and representativeness of the Service.

He was more than happy (but not surprised) when Senator Tom Connally as chairman of the Senate Foreign Relations Committee finally came forward in 1950 with the idea of establishing consultative subcommittees, paralleling the major bureaus of the Department of State. This made possible informal and off-the-record briefings and exchange of information between Assistant Secretaries and subcommittee members. This kept members of the Foreign Relations Committee abreast of world conditions and policy developments at a critical time. It also allowed the Department decision-makers to learn congressional sentiment at first hand.

Mass briefing conferences on a regular basis are no longer needed as most Congressmen have now been following foreign relations with some interest for a number of years. (Of course, a conference now and then wouldn't hurt.) The visits of Foreign Service officers to Capitol Hill have continued and are useful to Congress, to the Department, and to the Foreign Service officers themselves. The use of consultative subcommittees as a liaison device has fluctuated rather widely since its inception, but remains a useful means of liaison and now seems likely to survive.

Conclusions

The proper execution of the information and consultation functions of the Congressional Relations Area is as important to the Department as to the Congress, for no policy can exist for very long unless both understand and accept it, rather than having it imposed by either one upon the other. Congress cannot take a more enlightened view of foreign policy problems until the informational resources of the executive branch are made available to it in objective fashion, so that its members may accustom themselves to facing complex policy decisions with comprehension and sophistication.

Consultation is an adjunct of the information function, but is also important in its own right. Consultation need not threaten the role of the Department and the executive branch as the formulator and initiator of policy. It may lead to more judicious review of foreign relations questions by the Congress, to fewer violent differences of opinion which provoke the non-rational fluctuations in policy which disturb our allies and give comfort to those competing with us for world approval. A further exploration by both Congress and the Department of the possibilities for two-way consultation on opinions and ideas between them at a variety of levels in the development of foreign policy may be a positive step toward improving legislative-executive relations. ("Properly used" by the Department and "not abused" by the Congress, the consultative subcommittees can be a more useful device for encouraging an exchange of views between the executive and legislative branches of government.)

The development of a spirit of bipartisanship on questions of foreign policy, both within the Congress and particularly by the Department in its relationships with Congress when different parties control the two branches of government, may be a second positive step toward improving legislative-executive relations. A flowering of bipartisanship within Congress may appear at first to produce nothing more than congressional unity in opposition to the executive. On the other hand, the objective approach fostered by bipartisanship in Congress contributes to more rational negotiations between the two branches of government.

Many factors tend to limit growth of either consultation or bipartisanship as practical devices for reducing legislative-executive tensions in the foreseeable future. The legislative liaison specialists in the Congressional Relations Area have shown little disposition (and perhaps are in no position) to introduce any techniques which would alter in any fundamental way the relationships or respective roles of the legislative and executive branches in the policy-making process. One can hope that some progress will eventually be made toward further development of regular and effective consultative procedures between the Department and bipartisan foreign affairs leaders in Congress (long before executive decisions are finalized) without infringing in any way upon the executive responsibility for policy-making (which of necessity is more likely to increase than decrease in the future). Until such an evolution can occur, the legislative liaison staff will contribute mightily to the maintenance of satisfactory working relations between two participants with different but important roles in the formulation and conduct of American foreign policy.

6 Public Information Officers
Reaching Main Street

Sometimes it seems that the Department of State conducts foreign relations in a fishbowl. Representatives of the press prowl Department corridors, arrange interviews with policy officers without central clearance, report to the public with no censorship of copy. As guardians of the public interest in foreign policy, the free press often has access to information on possible responses to crisis situations while Department discussions are still in progress.

Such a privileged role places great responsibility upon the correspondents who cover the Department and its activities. The newsmen—whether from press, radio, or television—have an obligation to the public to report accurately what transpires within the Department's walls. Contrariwise, they must not reveal information which will endanger national security or jeopardize current negotiations with foreign powers.

To help the press get the news which can be properly released, public information officers in the Office of News in the Department's Bureau of Public Affairs maintain constant liaison with reporters of all major newspapers and press associations. Comfortable working quarters are maintained adjacent to the Office of News by the Department for the use of correspondents assigned to analyze foreign policy developments. Two restrictions introduced in 1958 brought howls of indignation from the press. Policy-making officers are now required to prepare a memorandum of conversation after being interviewed by a reporter. Proposed interviews with intelligence analysts must now be approved ahead of time by the Office of News.

116

While reporters still gather many stories individually and rather informally, the most dramatic formal source of news is the Secretary of State's weekly press conference. John Foster Dulles, when he became Secretary, elevated this event to new prominence by holding conferences regularly and by his willingness to comment more freely than some of his predecessors on most questions posed by correspondents.

Secretary Herter had not held many press conferences by March 1960, preferring to schedule the few he did conduct on Monday afternoons rather than on Tuesday mornings, the practice during the Dulles regime. The Monday conference necessitates preparation of briefing materials for the conference on the Friday before. As a result, some of the material is outdated by Monday morning —and other questions have come to the fore—so that additional materials must be gathered from the Department Monday morning for the Secretary's use. Secretary Dulles held his conferences on Tuesday, the day before the President's press conference, to get foreign affairs matters out of the way so the President wouldn't be bothered with them; Herter has been unwilling to assume this dominant role in a period when the President has taken over a considerable degree of leadership in the foreign affairs field.

Secretaries may come and go, but the procedures of preparation and even the conduct of the conference of necessity remain much the same. A present-tense description of what a Dulles conference was like will illustrate the processes involved and indicate why the press conference is important to the Department and the public.

THE SECRETARY'S PRESS CONFERENCE

The quiet tension in the State Department Auditorium is broken by a ripple of whispered comment. It is precisely 11 A.M. as Secretary of State Dulles strides down the center aisle, ready to face another forty minutes of tough questioning by Washington's top correspondents. Following him in a single file are Assistant Secretary for Public Affairs Andrew H. Berding and News Division Chief Lincoln White (who is now Director of the Office of News).

As the Secretary turns into position at the lectern, his assistants sink into flanking seats behind him. The flood lamps suddenly glare on from either side of the auditorium. Television and movie newsreel cameras whir from the rear. The Secretary looks up, pauses with eyebrows raised, then speaks. "I have a statement to read. . . ."

Secretary Dulles meets with the press almost every Tuesday morning he is in Washington. Newsmen hope successors continue to match this pace. Although crises and international conferences often take him abroad, the Secretary holds more press conferences than any other member of the Eisenhower cabinet. Second to those of the President himself, they are the best attended in the Capitol.

Secretary Dulles says, ". . . I am speaking not only to the press but I am speaking to the world at these press conferences." This is literally true, for among the 225 persons in the auditorium are representatives of press associations whose news services encircle the globe: Associated Press, United Press International, Reuters, and the German News Agency. There are reporters from *Tass, Le Monde,* and the *London Times,* from Japan and Israel, as well as from leading American papers and news magazines.

The humming cameras in the rear of the auditorium are an innovation. NBC and CBS crews are present. ABC and independent television stations are represented by Telenews. This coverage enables approximately 60,000,000 American TV viewers to see Secretary Dulles and hear brief excerpts from his remarks before midnight. The cameras of Hearst's Metrotone News, Twentieth Century Fox's Movietone News, Paramount News, and Universal-International News allow millions of theater-goers to get a quick glimpse and hear the voice of the Secretary within the week.

Secretary Dulles completes a 200-word opening statement on the situation in the Middle East. "Now if you have any questions." "Mr. Secretary, . . ." Three or four correspondents demand his attention at a single time as the question period opens. The Secretary is on his own. He carries no notes. His remarks are extemporaneous. How well he answers questions depends in part upon his own rich fund of information gleaned from years of experience as a top-level diplomat.

Secretary Dulles responds to a query concerning a discussion of the Japanese Peace Treaty with the Foreign Minister of Japan. "That clause was put in the treaty—I wrote the treaty very largely, as you may remember—for the very purpose of trying to prevent the Soviet Union from getting more favorable treatment than the United States got. I merely reminded the Japanese of the existence of that clause."

Questions are specific. They demand background knowledge of events which have broken during the past week or the last twenty-four hours. Too many "no comments" decrease the effectiveness of the press conference as a medium of information or diplomacy.

"Mr. Secretary, Mr. Churchill made a suggestion that under certain conditions Russia ought to be included in a kind of expanded NATO. . . . Could you comment . . . ?"

Secretary Dulles replies without hesitation. "I read quite carefully the text of what Sir Winston Churchill said. . . ."

How can one man know "everything," and be able to comment on the relevancy of any world event to American foreign policy? The staff work in the Department of State which goes into preparing the Secretary for the news conference is fascinating and essential. It enables Secretary Dulles to answer in some detail over 90 per cent of the questions thrown at him on camera by the best reporters in Washington; men like James Reston of the *New York Times*, Joseph Harsch of the *Christian Science Monitor*, Chalmers Roberts of the *Washington Post and Times Herald*, and John Hightower of Associated Press.

Central figures in the preparation of the Secretary for the news conference are the Assistant Secretary for Public Affairs and the Chief of the Office of News. Working as a team, they are tremendously effective. Andrew Berding, sworn in as Assistant Secretary replacing Carl W. McCardle, was a crack reporter for the Associated Press and an editorial writer for the *Buffalo Eve-*

ning News before entering government service. After compiling
a distinguished war record in the OSS (Office of Strategic Services), he served as director of information for the Department
of Defense, the Office of Defense Mobilization, and the Mutual
Security Administration. He came to the State Department from
a successful tour as Deputy Director of the United States Information Agency. Happy at his appointment with State after years
of experience in other agencies dealing with foreign policy and
national security affairs, Berding felt he was finally "getting
married after having had twins." Reporters have long considered
him one of the best press officers in government. His businesslike,
democratic approach endears him to newspapermen and co-
workers alike.

The Assistant Secretary for Public Affairs must concentrate on
what the columnists and commentators are saying. Critical comment on foreign policy in the press often foreshadows questions
at the next press conference. Berding, like McCardle before him,
keeps a weather eye out for potential questions on controversial
topics, pinpoints the hot potatoes, is adept at suggesting answers.

Carl McCardle's batting average during his four years as Assistant Secretary was good, but no one bats 1.000. At the height of
the threatened seizure of Quemoy and Matsu by the Chinese
Communists in April 1955, a certain State Department official
resigned under pressure from the Department. Secretary Dulles
was briefed on the case in perfunctory fashion, but he was not
prepared for the gruelling cross-examination to which he was
subjected at his news conference. Two-thirds of the questions
dealt with the affair; it consumed three-fourths of the time. With
some heat, Secretary Dulles finally declared, "I would think it
should be realized . . . that we are going through a period of
extreme tensity and danger in the international situation. . . .
If I should spend all the time that was necessary to know everything that was going on in relation to this . . . matter I should
be dismissed as Secretary of State of the United States."

Lincoln White presides over the Department's News Division
(now the Office of News), part of Berding's domain of Public

Affairs, and sometimes talks to reporters like a Dutch uncle. They bombard him with questions, accept him as one of their own. The tall Tennesseean, often quoted as an "official spokesman" in the press, is fitted for his role by two decades of experience with newsmen in the Department. Twenty-five reporters assigned to cover the Department attend his daily noon press conference. From formal questions and informal discussions, he knows what is of interest to them, what information they want.

Monday morning White works under great pressure. He attends the Secretary's regular 9:15 A.M. staff meeting with top advisers, to be kept abreast of current problems confronting the Department. He takes notes at the Secretary's big desk as Mr. Dulles leads discussion at the conference table. White checks with Berding as the meeting ends to find out if the press conference is on for Tuesday. Then he returns to the News Division to brief his own staff and to be alerted to divisional problems. Joseph Reap, his Assistant Chief (now Deputy Director of the Office of News), and others in the division suggest questions.

From here he proceeds to a briefing session with Public Affairs Area (now the Bureau of Public Affairs) representatives and public affairs advisers from the Department's geographic and functional bureaus. As he races through this schedule, he is developing in his mind and jotting down at odd intervals additional questions which may be posed to the Secretary by the press on Tuesday morning. With his third formal staff discussion of the morning under his belt some time between 11 A.M. and 1 P.M., White exchanges views at a fourth meeting with public affairs advisers about questions and answers for the Tuesday press conference. They return to their bureaus to request answers from the country desk officers to the questions suggested. He rushes to his noon press conference.[1]

With his morning merry-go-round completed, and after an all-too-brief lunch, White sits down at his typewriter to formal-

---

[1] Some Secretaries have excluded the representative of the Office of News from several morning staff conferences each week. This tends to make a proper daily briefing of the press very difficult.

ize the questions anticipated for Tuesday. "What would I tag the Old Man with?" He has a deep affection for the Boss. At some time between 2 and 4 P.M., he phones the public affairs advisers in appropriate bureaus and ticks off his list of questions. Each of five or more bureaus or areas in the Department are assigned two to four questions. Perhaps five specific queries are spelled out under particularly significant broad questions. There may be thirty questions in all.

Now the desk officers can complete their answers to questions passed on informally earlier and work out replies to any new ones included on White's formal list. An answer of from one to three pages is drawn up for each. Included are background information and a statement of the Department's attitude toward the situation involved. Pertinent documents may be attached. Replies are cleared with interested officers in the desk man's own or other bureaus and initialed by the Assistant or Deputy Assistant Secretaries concerned.

The goal is to have cleared answers back to the News Division rapidly enough so that they may be typed and collated for presentation to Secretary Dulles by 5:30 or 6 P.M. Copies also go to Berding and to White. The three men study this homework individually Monday evening. Normally, the entire list of questions and well over 50 per cent of the answers are in their briefcases as they leave the Department.

By Tuesday morning answers to all the questions developed through the News Division for the press conference are on the Secretary's desk. Mr. Dulles arrives at his office, studies the new material, and reads a special summary of the Department's incoming and outgoing cables for the past twenty-four hours. Officers of the Executive Secretariat reported in between 3 and 4 A.M. in order to place the tightly-knit summary in his hands by 8:30 A.M.

He attends the regular daily staff meeting with his advisers of Assistant Secretary level and above. The Director for Intelligence and Research leads off the briefing, presenting his five-to fifteen-minute distillation of the latest intelligence information. Analysts from the Bureau of Intelligence and Research come in shortly after 6 A.M. to assemble and analyze information, and to brief the Director between 8:20 and 9 A.M. The Chief of INR's Office of Research and Analysis for the Sino-Soviet Bloc gives his once-weekly round-up of developments and trends in the Soviet Union and other Communist-controlled countries. The Secretary takes an active interest in both briefings, often interjects questions.

Secretary Dulles starts with his Under Secretary, goes counter-clockwise around the conference table, giving each person an opportunity to raise problems for his or others' attention. If a problem demands immediate action, he appoints a group to meet during the morning to make a recommendation. The Secretary does not like to reach decisions on the spot without adequate staff work, and sometimes finds it necessary.

The briefing session at an end, Secretary Dulles reviews his homework for the press conference. At 10 A.M., he is joined by Berding and White. They quickly agree on the ten most likely questions. The Secretary does a dry run of answers. He has his own ideas of how he wants to handle them, and may discard a staff answer if he wishes. If either adviser sees bugs in the proposed replies, they tell him and may fill him in on details.

Shortly before 11 A.M., the Secretary enters his private elevator with his two aides and descends from the fifth to the second floor. He is just a few steps from the door to the rear entrance of the State Department Auditorium. From now on, he carries the ball alone. The Secretary knows the news conference will last forty minutes. During this period, he will answer eight to twelve major questions. Subordinate queries by reporters to fill in their stories may bring the total number to thirty or forty questions.

Secretary Dulles speaks indirectly to foreign government via the press conference. From February through April 1955, "Chi-Com" pressure on Formosa is increasing. Matsu and Quemoy are endangered. Reporters badger him at almost every news conference. "Mr. Secretary, do you believe that President Eisenhower would regard an attack on Quemoy and Matsu as an attack on Formosa?"

The Secretary invariably turns the question aside. "We have a commitment to defend the United States of America. But nobody yet has required us to state precisely what the means would be of defense in the event of certain types of attack which cannot be predicted. I repeat again and again and again—(*laughter*)— that our only commitment is to defend Formosa and the Pescadores and if there were no challenge to Formosa and the Pescadores, then there wouldn't be any question as far as we are concerned of fighting in that area."

Secretary Dulles believes in April 1955 that seven miles of open water stand between war and peace. He is trying to avoid another Korea. If he commits the United States to protect Quemoy and Matsu, the Chinese Communists may feel obliged to attack to prove their strength to the world. If he draws a line excluding them, another dreary evacuation like that of the Tachens may follow.

By June 1955, tension ebbs. "Would you say, Mr. Secretary, that there is in effect now a *de facto* cease-fire in the Formosa Straits, and is that a satisfactory solution for the time being?"

Secretary Dulles: "I think you could fairly call it a *de facto* cease-fire. Of course, it is not satisfactory to have it be on as informal a basis as it now is, but . . . sometimes things are dealt with better . . . on a quite informal basis, and to attempt to formalize them raises problems which are very difficult to get over."

In December 1955, an enterprising reporter reopens the question. "Sir, it is a long time since we have heard about the Islands of Quemoy and Matsu. . . ." The Secretary brushes off the query. "Well, I doubt very much if it would serve any useful purpose to resurrect the issues about those islands, which . . . have happily subsided into the background. I think that . . . is a good place to leave them for the time being."

It is persistent May Craig, representing assorted Maine newspapers, who finally smokes the Secretary out in mid-January 1956. "Mr. Secretary, you have just said that our views should be made clear lest the enemy miscalculate and get into war. Why do we not make our position clear on Matsu and Quemoy?"

Secretary Dulles: "I think it is clear."

Mrs. Craig: "It is not clear to me, sir."

Secretary Dulles: "It is not clear to you because you, like me, cannot read the minds of the Chinese Communists. But to them I think it is quite clear."

Mrs. Craig: "What do you think they think we mean to do?"

Secretary Dulles: "I think that they think that if an attack is started there which comprehends a claim to take by force Formosa and the Penghus, that we will fight."

Although the international scene is often somber and foreign policy a serious matter, press conferences are not without their lighter moments.

The Secretary is under fire for planning to go to San Francisco to help his party draft its 1956 platform statement on foreign affairs.

Question: "Do you think it is possible to write a bipartisan plank on foreign policy?"

Secretary Dulles: "That depends on the Democrats. If they agree I could write one."

Question: "Have they invited you to their convention?"

Secretary Dulles: "No, but they still may. It would be a very good idea. I would be delighted to go."

In March 1957, heralding the approach of Spring, the Secretary declares himself in favor of true love:

Question: "Mr. Secretary, Harold Connolly, the United States Olympic hammer-throw champion, is reported that way about a Czech lady discus thrower. (*Laughter.*) And he has appealed to the Czech government for permission to get her out, marry her, and bring her to this country. Is the United States government making any appeals to back up his appeal?"

Secretary Dulles: "Well, we believe in romance." (*Laughter.*)

Gradually as the conference continues the process of securing the floor becomes more ordered. Every reporter with a question has an opportunity to ask it.

"Thank you, Mr. Secretary." John Hightower, Pulitzer-prize-winning senior correspondent at the Department of State, brings the conference to a close. Newsmen break into the aisles in a fast heel and toe, headed for the telephones. Within sixty seconds, fleet-footed reporters are dictating their first leads from notes scribbled during the question period. Minutes later the early stories on the news conference are coming in over the AP and UPI news tickers in the press branch of the Department's News Division. The Secretary has spoken to the world.

Some question the wisdom of such public diplomacy. Pressure from the press certainly brings public disclosure of much information which would not otherwise be revealed. It sometimes forces the formulation of policy on a problem that might otherwise have been "swept under the rug." Successful use of the press conference requires wise choices of when, how, and what to disclose. The Dulles record on these scores is not bad—considering time pressures and the sharpness of the questioning—but it is far from perfect.

In explaining the Department's position to the press, the Secretary finds an occasional informal press conference a valuable supplement to the formal Tuesday news conference. He may dine with ten to twenty of the most responsible newsmen in Washington and frankly discuss important questions under consideration by the Department of State. Correspondents make no attribution of these remarks, but they gain an understanding of problems which enables them to cover the Department and the Tuesday conferences in more detail, with greater accuracy. This builds public knowledge of American foreign policy both at home and overseas.

In praising Secretary Dulles for being "most conscientious" in keeping the public informed, J. R. Wiggins, executive editor of the *Washington Post and Times Herald,* declares: "Individual citizens may be able to say that they do not agree with the policies or methods of the Secretary. They cannot fairly say that they do not know what they are. This is not to say that these policies escape criticism. The criticism, whatever it is, can be based on full information, and this has not always been so."

Public discussion of basic foreign policy issues is important to the progressive growth of democratic processes. For his contributions toward this end (through his relations with the daily press and the fast media), citizens may well say, "Thank you, Mr. Secretary."

WANTED: PUBLIC UNDERSTANDING

Public understanding of foreign policy doesn't grow on apple trees in Indiana orchards. Nor would seven press conferences a week by the Secretary of State arouse much interest in policy among the potato farmers of upstate New York. The Secretary's press conference and the Department's daily relations with the press through the Office of News make the first impact of public opinion when a new question of foreign policy arises. The shot is heard round the world, but the Secretary's words fall harmlessly like spent bullets on major segments of the domestic population.

Americans deeply interested in foreign policy constitute a dedicated few. As for the rest, in varying degrees, "they've gone fishin'," until the bold black headlines or staccato-voiced announcers tell them their lives are threatened or their pocketbooks pinched. However, the percentage of citizens continuously aware of policy problems, trying desperately to comprehend the complexities of world relationships, is higher today than a decade ago. Portions of the press have contributed notably to this improvement, as have patriotic community leaders in town and countryside across America.

There are thousands of intellectuals who read the verbatim accounts of the Secretary's press conference in the *New York Times;* others, who enjoy the excellent summaries prepared by John Hightower of Associated Press. These are the people— lawyers, ministers, journalists, businessmen, teachers, and students—to whom the public information specialists in the Public

Services and Historical Offices of the Bureau of Public Affairs address the bulk of their attention.

"Foreign policy isn't just something that's conducted by secretaries of state and by ambassadors; every one of you has got a part in making a successful foreign policy for the United States," Dulles once said. He was right. Public support for policy is a necessity in the age of alliances, overseas aid, and rocket-propelled H-bombs.

As discussions begin among thoughtful Americans in the wake of the Secretary's press conference or stirring international events reported on the front pages of the nations's press, there is need for a follow-through in greater depth to explain the Department's position.

The Department is one of the few great agencies of the government which lacks a built-in interest group to support its policies (if they are in accord with what the constituents think back home). Commerce, Labor, and Agriculture are the clearest examples of having what State has not. (Of course, this cozy relationship can backfire. State should perhaps be thankful that the pressures upon it are often contradictory.) State Department information specialists do face a tough task, though, as they try to consult and influence public opinion at a wide variety of leadership levels, which is their job in the intricate cooperative venture of formulating and conducting foreign policy.

Citizens can't really help decide what sort of policy may be best for the United States if they don't know what policy is now and what it has been. Yet, how many Americans can even begin to answer the following questions? What are the contemporary policies of our nation in North Africa, the Middle East, toward Poland and Hungary? What does the Secretary think are the prospects for de-Stalinization or re-Stalinization in the Soviet Union? For a summit conference? What are the trends of policy in the Far East? What was policy in the past toward each of these areas or problems? Do past relations narrow the range of present practical alternatives?

Enlightened public opinion based on facts, setting rational limits to action, can contribute to the development of foreign policies which are in the long-range national interest. Acquisition of such knowledge by the general public requires sustained interest by organizations and individuals, and calls for community discussion in cities and towns throughout the length and breadth of the land.

THE OFFICE OF PUBLIC SERVICES

The work of the Office of Public Services in the Bureau of Public Affairs is a major part of the Department's program for creating greater understanding of American foreign policy. Public information officers maintain working relations with many national non-governmental organizations, like Rotary International or the League of Women Voters. The major functions of the Office are to provide speakers for groups desiring to schedule foreign policy discussions, to answer letters from thousands of citizens requesting information or giving advice on foreign affairs, to publish a wide range of pamphlets for public distribution to groups or individuals actively interested in contemporary American foreign policy, and to maintain liaison with national organizations.

Through four organization liaison specialists, who deal on a daily basis with representatives of national organizations or interest groups, the Office of Public Services contributes to an exchange of facts and ideas which lead to an accommodation between the views of the Department of State and the organizations concerned. Liaison officers are in close contact with the executive directors and headquarters staffs of such groups, attend national conventions of organizations interested in foreign policy, provide Department speakers for these conventions, arrange for briefings in the Department of national officers or delegations visiting Washington, and provide material from the Department for publications of these groups. One liaison officer (a woman) deals with women's, educational, and youth groups; a second, with veterans and fraternal groups; a third, with religious, men's service, and business groups; and a fourth, with labor and international relations organizations.

The liaison with national organizations is a fruitful two-way street. It provides an opportunity for the members of these groups through their leaders to bring influence to bear on American foreign policy. Conversely, the exchange allows the Department's views to be channeled to millions of Americans. (Department publications are usually limited to press runs of 20,000 to 40,000 copies, but a single reprint in the publication of a national organization may reach over 1,000,000 citizens.)

Citizens groups make over sixteen hundred requests for speakers from the Department each year. These are processed by the Office of Public Services. Over a thousand speaking engagements are actually filled. They are scheduled from one to three months in advance. Influential national organizations receive high priority. The odds are favorable to smaller groups if they are able to come to Washington or the Department for conferences. Although six hundred out-of-town talks are made in a year, the chances of securing a Department speaker fade in direct proportion to the number of miles from the nation's Capitol. More than two hundred speeches per year are made in the East, about eighty in the Far West. Department officers make as many as thirteen appearances on a swing to the West Coast. A speaker scheduled for a larger city may be routed to a smaller community if local program dates can be fitted into his travel plans.

The Department has no hired speech-makers. The representatives who talk before local groups perform this task in addition to their regular duties. The Department is anxious to get its employees out to meet the people on Main Street, and feels that it helps policy-makers understand public opinion. The first choice of most local groups seeking a speaker from the Department is (at very least) an Assistant Secretary of State. The plain fact of the matter is that there just aren't enough of them to go around. The few of them who do exist are too busy most of the time to go traipsing across the country giving speeches—unless there is a real public opinion brush fire in some spot threatening rational consideration of policy. Groups sincerely interested in foreign policy can better their chances of securing a Department speaker by settling for expertise alone, rather than insisting upon rank as well.

A panel discussion is typical of community forum programs. No one participant has much time to talk, which keeps those present awake. Adding names to the list of participants helps to drum up an audience in the first place, as any organization program chairman knows. The Department can't afford the luxury of this type of cooperation. Foreign policy is a complex topic. Explaining the why of policy takes time. There is the inevitable question period. Most Department speakers are Foreign Service officers or civil servants who should not have to debate current controversial issues with other panel members, since their role is to execute the agreed government position whatever may be their own personal beliefs.

Individual citizens asking questions or wishing to express opinions on foreign policy write over 100,000 letters per year to Congressmen, the Secretary of State, and the President. These letters are channeled through Public Correspondence in the Office of Public Services.[2] Answers usually clear the Department in less than two weeks. Each Friday, a weekly analysis of opinion expressed in these letters is sent to public affairs advisers in all the bureaus of the Department. The analysis even goes into the weekend reading folder of the Secretary of State. A one-page summary, with some evaluation and interpretation, the analysis may include a pro and con count on a simple issue or indicate the number of letters supporting each of fifteen different views on a more complex question.

Good advice (which most people don't need) is "Don't write

---

[2] Recent fiscal year figures were 127,500 letters in 1956; 118,316 in 1957; and 35,496 in 1958. The drop in FY 1958 over the other years is attributed to the absence of international crises or events such as Suez, Hungary, etc., which elicited highly emotional public responses in FY 1956 and FY 1957. The volume from July 1, 1958, to the end of 1958 jumped; some 56,032 pieces of correspondence were received in the last six months of the year (the first half of FY 1959).

every day." "Regulars," with a penchant for armchair diplomacy, account for about 200 incoming letters each week. If you beat the donkey (or elephant) too often, the stick loses its effectiveness. Letters get the attention they deserve. A printed handout prepared by an interest group, complete with the Department's address stamped on the card or envelope, gets a similarly canned answer. Thousands of such cards do not outweigh a single thoughtful letter from an individual or an organization secretary, posing problems and asking for information. Letters are thoroughly sorted to determine the level of reply.

A unique question or opinion requires a special answer. A rough draft of the reply is written by a drafting officer in the Office of Public Services. He is a specialist in the area of interest to the letter writer. His reply is often read and revised by a country desk officer in a regional action bureau of the Department. The letter is cleared, perhaps by an Assistant Secretary of State, so that it becomes an official statement of American foreign policy.

Hundreds of persons often write asking the Department the same question. Because of the widespread interest in the point raised, the reply is given careful attention. It is reviewed word by word in two or more bureaus and at a variety of levels. Then an electrotyped form letter or printed statement is forwarded explaining the Department's position. About 75 per cent of the letters received are answered this way.

The Office of Public Services publishes leaflets or pamphlets on many topics of general interest. These are often pertinent enclosures in letters of reply. The Office has a limited number of publications for free distribution. They are also made available through the Superintendent of Documents in the Government Printing Office for a small fee. Leaflets describe "Your Department of State," "The American Consul," "The American Ambassador," and "The Agricultural Attaché." Brief but understandable pamphlets tell about such diversified topics as "The Foreign Service of the United States," "How Foreign Policy is Made," "Disarmament: The Intensified Effort, 1955–1958," "The International Cultural Relations of the United States," and "The Soviet Note on Berlin: An Analysis." Foreign policy speeches of the Secretary of State and the President are often reprinted and issued by the Office.

The *Background* publications are of use to laymen. Published irregularly, they often discuss a country, but on occasion they cover events or policies. Sample titles are "Thailand," "Malaya," "Ceylon," "Three New African Nations: Morocco, Tunisia, Libya," or the "United Nations General Assembly." *Background* tells something of the geography and history of a country, as well as facts about production and trade. Relationships with neighboring areas and to American foreign policy are stressed. Similar to *Background*, but briefer and limited to describing International Cooperation Administration programs abroad, is *Fact Sheet*. Among current titles for distribution are "Tunisia," "Afghanistan," and "Thailand."

Appearing regularly are the weekly *Department of State Bulletin* and the fortnightly *Foreign Policy Briefs*. The *Bulletin* features articles by Department officers on current topics, official statements of policy, and the texts of resolutions or recent treaties. *Briefs* contains interesting and unusual information on foreign policy of value to editors of organization publications or weekly newspapers.

Altogether, the Department distributes some 300 current titles to citizens seeking information on foreign policy. Some 10,000 individuals and organizations have asked to receive one or more Department publication regularly; mailing lists based on requests include newspapers, radio and television stations, school libraries, professors, clergymen, and leaders of many private organizations, both large and small. (Of course, 10,000 is a pitifully small number out of approximately 180,000,000 Americans.)

THE HISTORICAL OFFICE

Present policies have roots in the past. Serious students of foreign policy find the Historical Office of the Department's Bureau of Public Affairs of particular interest. Its staff, composed of historians and researchers, prepares historical narratives which set contemporary policies in perspective (both for policy-makers and the public), publishes basic diplomatic documents, and gives assistance to researchers analyzing past or present policies of the United States.

A number of Department publications which include historical background are prepared in the Historical Office and distributed by Public Services. One of these is "The Department of State: 1930 to 1955," a description of the Department's growth, organization, and how it functions. Collections of documents on international conferences are released for ready reference by organization discussion leaders, newsmen, and students of foreign policy. An example is "The Suez Problem, July 26 to September 21, 1956." The Historical Office also engaged in tripartite publication, with Great Britain and France, of documents captured from the German foreign office during World War II.

Considerable public use has been made of the Division's *Foreign Relations of the United States*, published since 1861. This series is available in most college or municipal libraries, contains invaluable source material for research by lawyers, courts, professors, and Department officers (if they have the time). *Foreign Relations* is a relatively solid documentation of American diplomatic history. It does not try to gloss over policy mistakes. All volumes through 1939 have been published. Compilation is complete through 1944. A more contemporary if less complete documentary publication was the Office's *American Foreign Policy, 1950–1955*.

Scholars or ordinary individuals with a more than average interest in some special topic from all over the United States go directly to primary sources in Washington to study detailed aspects of foreign policy. State Department files are generally open for such study through 1929, with limited access to records up to 1942. Over 1,000 requests are made each year by individuals or research groups to the Historical Office for information from or access to Department records, or for review of manuscripts (over 18,000 typewritten pages per year) based on them.

The Department of State provides information on foreign policy for almost any interested Americans (of which there are not a sufficient number). The millions who read the newspapers or watch television absorb the first impact of the Department's information program, but are rarely staggered. Thousands of others, as individuals or as members of groups, follow up current news with an attempt to place contemporary events in sharper analytical or historical focus.

The primary purpose of the Department's public information program is clear. It is to tell what policies are and to explain why they have been adopted. Such information is important. It is the basis of useful discussion. No democratic checks on policy-makers can exist without public knowledge of the whats and whys of foreign policy.

National organizations such as the Foreign Policy Association, the American Association for the United Nations, and the Council on Foreign Relations also perform an information function and present facts. In addition—something the Department's information program cannot do—they have an obligation to raise issues and stimulate discussion by presenting alternative policies and justifications. Public discussion is most fruitful when there is knowledge of policy and of possible alternatives.

Government information programs on foreign policy in democracies must be kept in cooperative balance with those of private agencies. If unlimited funds were provided for public information, public opinion might be overwhelmed and consideration of policy alternatives cease. When government funds are too limited, individuals and organizations may find it difficult to know what policies are. There is a delicate balance between too much and too little.

The State Department's public information program is probably not far from the golden mean. Its funds and personnel were severely cut in 1953. There has been some regrowth since, but public pressure for information (particularly for speakers) remains partially unsatisfied. While this is preferable to satiation—

because Americans can discuss among themselves without complete dependence upon the Department—many people are not interested in policy because they are not contacted by either the government or private organizations. The competition for their attention from other less disturbing sources is terrific.

The big problem for the Department is breaking the barrier of the city of 150,000 and explaining policy to citizens in smaller communities. Increased cooperation between the Department and local chapters of national organizations could help reach the grass roots but would require additional funds for fielding speakers. Such a program, however, would tend to enlarge the number of persons with at least a minimum if uncritical understanding of foreign policy.

The State Department's public information program seeks to encourage public understanding of and support for foreign policy in cities and towns from the Atlantic to the Pacific, from Canada to the Gulf of Mexico. In doing this, it makes a valuable but definitely limited contribution to the continued existence of the democratic way of life.

7 Public Opinion Analysts
Voice of the People

EVERYBODY'S BUSINESS

In the "Model T days" of American diplomacy (whose closing date can be argued by historians), Department of State policymakers rattled over the bumpy roads of foreign relations more as sight-seers than men of action, lost in the dust of the British Rolls-Royce which set the pace in foreign affairs. They rarely excited the attention of the broad membership of Congress or the general domestic public. If restless outlanders threw stones from time to time, they usually aimed at the powerful Rolls-Royce rather than at the old Model T.

These days are long since gone. The sleek black Cadillac, symbolizing contemporary American diplomacy with its highly complex policy-making mechanism, draws critical attention at home and abroad. The concept of total diplomacy evolved in the post-World War II period, involving heavy expenditures for overseas military and economic assistance and a "combat-ready" defense force in time of peace, has made foreign policy everybody's business. As Secretary of State George Catlett Marshall said, "no policy—foreign or domestic—can succeed without public support."

Today there is no department or agency in the government more sensitive to American "public opinion" than the Department of State. Within the Department, the major responsibility for ascertaining the character of that public opinion as it concerns the formulation and conduct of foreign policy is assigned to public opinion analysts on the Public Opinion Studies Staff of the Bureau of Public Affairs. Their operations determine in large

137

measure whether or not decision-makers and policy-planners from the country desk level to the Secretary of State, as well as Foreign Service officers and USIA representatives in Washington or overseas, have an adequate picture of American public opinion on any foreign policy question. Under these circumstances, an understanding of the function and organization of the Staff and of its public opinion analysts becomes important.

FUNCTION

The function of the Public Opinion Studies Staff and its analysts is to place accurate summaries of American public opinion before officers of the United States government who are responsible for the formulation and conduct of foreign policy. The extent to which individual officers take such knowledge and integrate it into their considerations in the planning of policy would be difficult to assess accurately. The Staff queries Department officers, foreign posts, and other government agencies from time to time concerning their desire to continue to receive its summaries and reports. There have been numerous opportunities for officials to indicate that the Staff's work was not useful. However, quite to the contrary, the Staff's summaries and reports are becoming more popular.

The uses to which public opinion information prepared by the Staff is put depends upon the needs of the person receiving it. This is related to the function of his job. If the Policy Planning Staff requests information on some element of public opinion, this is evidence that such opinion is being given consideration on a reasonably broad or relatively long-range planning level and may be placed before the National Security Council. If geographic or functional bureaus request special summaries, it may indicate consideration on a more specific or short-range basis. Overseas, American representatives need to know if American public opinion agrees or disagrees with opinion in the country where the post is located. Knowledge of similarities and differences can be useful in diplomatic negotiations; information officers can be more tactful in carrying out the USIA program.

The Assistant Secretary of State for Public Affairs needs to know public, organization, press, and congressional opinion in his role as adviser on public information matters to the Secretary of State. That the late Secretary of State John Foster Dulles placed some importance upon knowing the realities of American opinion on any given aspect of policy was indicated by the increased emphasis on such responsibilities assigned to the Assistant Secretary for Public Affairs after 1953. Interest in public opinion at the White House level is shown by the coordination of State Department summaries of American public opinion and USIA summaries of public opinion abroad for use during the 1955 Geneva Conference.

The rise of the National Security Council, where coordination is sought on policies affecting national security between interested departments and agencies, has increased the importance of the Public Opinion Studies Staff to government officials outside the Department of State. Dissemination of its summaries and reports gives the participating departments and agencies additional common ground in their search for solutions of national security problems.

ORGANIZATION AND PERSONNEL

In view of the importance usually attributed to "public opinion" in a democracy, it is surprising to find how small the Public Opinion Studies Staff really is. It has only twelve staff members. Headed by its Director, the Staff consists of seven other opinion analysts. It is also served by the radio monitor, a hectograph operator, one typist and the Director's secretary. The Staff is organized on a geographic and functional basis, with each opinion analyst responsible for several geographic or functional areas of interest. One concentrates on general foreign policy and upon the Far East; another, on Russia, eastern Europe, refugees, and Latin America. A third analyst handles Germany, Austria, NATO, and western Europe; a fourth, the Middle East, north Africa, and southern Asia. Other analysts concentrate on functional problems. One deals with material on the Department of State and foreign trade; another, on organizations, the United Nations, atomic affairs, and disarmament. Each public opinion analyst is responsible for surveying from two to five daily papers and from six to eleven periodicals with the purpose of clipping and forwarding to each of his fellow analysts the articles which pertain to their areas of responsibility.

Personnel changes are not frequent among analysts in the Public Opinion Studies Staff. Personnel stability is essential. Almost a year's training on the job is required for an analyst to reach full efficiency. The work of the Staff constitutes a rather narrow specialization of technique and subject matter. As a result, there are no other jobs in government closely related to those on the Staff, no similar positions with higher salaries in other agencies to drain off personnel. This tends to minimize turnover problems.

Staff personnel are not to be integrated into the Foreign Service because of the degree of specialization in their work. Foreign Service officers, who might have been rotated through the Staff if "Wristonization" had been applied there, would not be "experts" on American public opinion. Nor would they be likely to remain on the Staff long enough to develop such a speciality.

Analysts have joined the Staff at GS-5 [1] or at higher levels and have promotion opportunities comparable to other Department divisions engaged in professional work. The Chief, who has served on the Staff since 1943, is a GS-15.[2] Not all analysts are college graduates, but several hold even M.A. or Ph.D. degrees.

SOURCES FOR DETERMINING PUBLIC OPINION

There are a variety of sources from which information concerning public opinion may be gathered. Most of them are of more value in determining the opinion of a certain public than of discovering public opinion as a whole. It is necessary for the Department of State and the Public Opinion Studies Staff to consider the opinions of both individual "publics" and the general

[1] This is the normal "general schedule grade" assigned to a college graduate entering into the Civil Service.

[2] This was formerly the top-ranking grade in the Civil Service. Now there are three super-grades in addition: GS-16, GS-17 and GS-18.

public. Three sources of public opinion which are readily available to the Department, and of great importance to it, are statements by members of Congress, by leaders of private organizations or interest groups, and by individuals who may write letters
to the White House or the Secretary of State.

The Congressional Relations Area is responsible for maintaining liaison between the Department and members of the Senate
and House. Primary responsibility for covering public expressions
by members of Congress as they may concern foreign policy is
within the province of the Public Opinion Studies Staff. Relations
with private organizations are the function of Organization Liaison
in the Office of Public Services in the Bureau of Public Affairs.
The Public Opinion Studies Staff of the Bureau is responsible
for summarizing opinions expressed publicly by representatives of
private organizations or interest groups. Letters are received,
answered, and analyzed through Public Correspondence in the
Office of Public Services. The analyses of opinions in letters received by Public Correspondence personnel are forwarded to the
Public Opinion Studies Staff for its consideration.

No one of these three sources of public opinion is an adequate
mirror of the pattern of opinion actually held by the American
people on any given date. They are, however, indicators and are
of importance in maintaining relations with Congress, with private
organizations, and with individuals interested in foreign policy.
They make a contribution toward filling in the over-all picture
of what public opinion may be, but they are not sufficient within
themselves to meet the needs of the Department of State.

Probably the best indicator available on a day-to-day basis of
over-all public opinion is the material which may be gleaned
from the press and periodicals, from radio and television. The
words of representative editorial writers, columnists, and commentators very quickly spell out the major positions which will
be taken by the press on a question of foreign policy. These
opinion leaders do not necessarily influence the fundamental beliefs of the American people on matters of foreign policy, but
they have reflected public opinion on most issues since the crea-

tion of the Public Studies Division in 1943. Although the Division became the present Public Opinion Studies Staff in November of 1959, the titular change indicated no change in function for the new Staff.

The best means for understanding the thinking of the general public remains the oft-maligned nationwide opinion poll. Its findings often confirm the picture obtained from analysis of the press. The original Public Studies Division had the benefit of periodic foreign policy polls conducted for it by public opinion research centers in leading universities from 1943 to 1957. Dependence upon the poll as a device for determining public opinion was never complete, because limitations of time and cost precluded the use of national polls on a daily basis.

PROCEDURES FOR GATHERING INFORMATION AND REPORTING

1. *Radio and Television*

Each weekday morning at 8:45 when the Director of the Public Opinion Studies Staff, H. Schuyler Foster, reports to work he finds on his desk major excerpts from radio and television comments of the preceding evening on foreign policy questions or the Department of State. By mid-morning the comments are on the desks of appropriate Department officers. Copies also go to analysts within the Staff for use, along with other newly-received opinion materials, in the *Daily Opinion Summary*. During a single week the regularly scheduled broadcasts of twenty-one commentators and three interview or discussion programs are monitored. These include broadcasts by all four major networks. Transcriptions are made each night except Saturday. The bulk of the comment is taken between 5:55 and 8 P.M. The monitoring program was re-established in 1956 after several years' absence because of budgetary problems. It has proven helpful to the Staff, because it allows some voices to be heard which are not available in the press, and it affords a fuller and quicker picture of American opinion than can be secured from other sources alone.

2. *Press and Periodicals*

When the public opinion analysts report each weekday morning, their first task is to read and clip "key" newspapers. Each analyst will read one or two papers, clip items bearing on foreign policy, the United Nations, or the Department of State, and distribute the items found to the analyst who specializes in that particular field. Each analyst studies the items he receives from the press and those from the monitoring service in his areas of interest to determine which of his fields may require coverage in that day's issue of the one- to three-page *Daily Opinion Summary*. Material not suitable for the daily may appear later in a weekly, monthly, area, or special summary.

By noon the material for the *Daily Opinion Summary* must be in and edited by Dr. Foster. By 1:30 P.M. it has been hectographed and distributed along with the *Secret Summary* prepared by the Executive Secretariat for the Department's 130 top officials. It also goes on a daily basis to 270 additional officers in the Department, or other government agencies who have requested it. The *Daily Opinion Summary* indicates the position of the writers or commentators and quotes enough to give the flavor or general feeling expressed. Experience has demonstrated that a press sample based upon papers received in Washington on the day of publication reflects rather accurately the pattern of opinion expressed in other newspapers across the country. Two dozen papers are acquired by the Staff and seventy-six additional newspapers are covered by a clipping service.

The Staff has found major schools of thought to be represented in a press sample which includes the *New York Times, New York Herald Tribune, New York Journal-American* (Hearst), *Philadelphia Inquirer, Baltimore Sun, Chicago Tribune, Washington Post and Times Herald, Washington Star,* and *Washington News* (Scripps-Howard). Comments may be a little stronger here and there, one way or the other, but are essentially the same in other newspapers consulted. These blanket the country from Spokane to Savannah, from Los Angeles to Boston, and from New Orleans to Minneapolis.

With the work on the *Daily Opinion Summary* completed, the analysts turn to preparation of materials for other publications of the Staff. These include a nine- to eleven-page *Monthly Survey of American Opinion on International Affairs,* five additional regularly-issued more detailed summaries, and special reports. In addition to radio and press comment already summarized for the *Daily Opinion Summary,* analysts must digest materials from the other newspapers, from forty-eight general periodicals and three newsletters, from the publications of some sixty private organizations, and the results of foreign policy polls.

The twenty-four periodicals acquired by the Staff and the twenty-four routed through it by the Department of State Library Division would appear to be representative of almost every element of American public opinion. Among others there are *Business Week* and the *New Republic,* the *Atlantic Monthly* and the *Saturday Evening Post, Harper's Magazine* and the *Reader's Digest, Newsweek* and *Time, Life* and *Look,* the *Christian Century* and *Commonweal, Nation's Business* and the *Reporter.* Ten of the periodicals are devoted primarily to questions of foreign policy and international relations: *Far Eastern Survey, Foreign Affairs,* the *Foreign Policy Bulletin,* the *Foreign Service Journal, Freedom and Union,* the *Hispanic-American Report, International Conciliation,* the *Journal of International Affairs, Pacific Affairs,* and *World Politics.*

Private organizations and interest groups are well represented in publications analyzed by the Staff. They fall under six categories: international relations, economic, women's, men's, veterans', and religious groups. Examples include, respectively, the Council on Foreign Relations, the American Farm Bureau Federation, the League of Women Voters, Rotary International, the American Legion, and the American Baptist Convention. The press and general periodicals often carry articles expressing the views of these organizations or their leaders. Many of the interest groups publish house organs which are made available to the Staff. Organization opinion is of particular interest to the Office of Public Services.

3. *Polls*

The published polls taken on a national or state basis are of real value to the Public Opinion Studies Staff in determining public opinion on foreign policy questions. Results of Dr. George Gallup's polls are released to the Staff at the same time as to the press. This is the only national poll published on a continuing basis. Most useful of the state polls is the Minnesota Poll, sponsored by Cowles Publications, which appears each Sunday in the *Minneapolis Tribune.* Of interest, but containing fewer questions concerning foreign affairs, is the Iowa Poll, also by Cowles Publications, published in the *Des Moines Register.* The Texas Poll, taken by Joe Belden, a commercial pollster, is of value but appears only sporadically. The Staff has discovered that the Minnesota Poll comes very close in indicating public opinion throughout the nation on the questions it covers. The Staff has found no significant sectional differences of opinion on foreign policy questions. These facts are confirmed by the geographic breakdowns of the Gallup Poll and of national polls undertaken by university-related public opinion research centers.

The Department of State, between 1943 and 1957, at one time or another contracted to secure polling data from the Office of Public Opinion Research at Princeton University, the Survey Research Center at the University of Michigan, and the National Opinion Research Center at the University of Chicago. Prior to 1957 and 1958, the Department was receiving the results of half-a-dozen such nationwide polls per year. The university polls usually covered from twelve to twenty questions, some of which were repeated periodically so that trends of opinion could be charted. Many questions asked were quite helpful to those directing the formulation and conduct of foreign policy in the Department of State. Queries were on such topics as trade, immigration, the Suez crisis, or on attitudes toward over-all foreign policy.

From 1948 to 1957, when the contract was terminated because of congressional discontent, public opinion polls (contracted under confidential funds of the Department for internal use among appropriate agencies of the executive branch) were conducted by the National Opinion Research Center at the University of Chicago. An inadvertent leak of poll figures to the press through public information officers in the International Co-operation Administration resulted in an investigation of the Department's polling techniques by the International Operations Subcommittee of the House Committee on Government Operations in June and July, 1957. The International Cooperation Administration was alleged to have used polling results for purposes of publicity or propaganda, prohibited by Section 701 of Public Law 603, Eighty-fourth Congress. In response to congressional criticism, even before the formal hearings were held, the Department cancelled the polling contract.

The knowledge acquired over a fourteen-year period within the Public Studies Division (predecessor of the present Public Opinion Studies Staff) concerning the relationship of public opinion as expressed by Department polls to opinion expressed in representative American newspapers, in Congress, and by Dr. Gallup's polls, still enables analysts to project what polling results might be for a brief time (even though Department polls are not conducted). There is no current interest among top Department officials in restoring the poll as a device for sampling public opinion, but its loss will be increasingly felt as issues change and projection becomes more difficult. (The polls contracted by the Department cost no more than $43,200 per year at the time of cancellation.) Congressional opposition to the polls stemmed from fear that the executive branch would use poll figures to influence opinion, so that public pressures would be brought to bear on Congress for appropriations to implement programs with strong public support—a strange problem in the world's leading democracy.

On the basis of past experience, public opinion polls (either those taken by Dr. Gallup or those formerly conducted by the NORC for the Department) often seem to be more favorable to a particular element of foreign policy than do congressional opinions. For example, a poll may indicate that 87 per cent of the American people favor foreign aid to nations which are allied with us. Votes in Congress are less overwhelming. This may be explained in part by the fact that the public is reacting to a generalization or principle, while the Congress is judging a detailed set of provisions. The people favor foreign assistance, but they have not strenuously objected on some occasions when appropriation requests have been cut by as much as a billion dollars.

Results of public opinion polls are often more favorable to a particular foreign policy than an analysis of the letters written to government officials would indicate. Generally, such an analysis has shown opposition to compulsory military training. Yet, over a sixteen-year period, Dr. Gallup has found in his polls that 70 per cent or more of the people are in favor of such training.

Statements by organization leaders as quoted or carried in the press may sometimes give readers a misleading impression of public opinion. During 1951 and 1952, newspaper and periodical items concerning organization resolutions which disparaged United States participation in the United Nations seemed to indicate the possibility of a change in public opinion from internationalism back to isolationism. But when the results of contemporary opinion polls came in, they demonstrated that 75 per cent or more of the general public continued to support United States membership in the United Nations.

Polls on a large number of topics show that the public took the same side as the columnists and the press on about four out of five foreign policy issues during the period from 1943 to 1952. The discrepancies occurred on novel questions or in instances where a strong personality was involved. For example, about nine out of ten columnists favored a three and three-quarter billion dollar postwar loan to Britain, but about 45 per cent of the general public were opposed to the loan and only about 35 per cent supported it. Again, the bulk of the commentators accepted President Harry Truman's action in the dismissal of General Douglas MacArthur, although some said that it should have been done in a less objectionable manner. A majority of the general public believed that MacArthur's dismissal was a mistake.

Members of the press and columnists may be better informed on questions of foreign policy than most members of the general public. They have more facts at hand and see many more broad relationships than does the average individual. This accounts in part for the occasional difference between attitudes expressed in press comment and those registered in opinion polls. The possibility of such a difference necessitates Public Opinion Studies Staff reports which present both press summaries and polls.

4. *Periodical Reports and Special Summaries*

The most widely distributed report of the Public Opinion Studies Staff is the *Monthly Survey of American Opinion on International Affairs*. Approximately 262 copies are routed to officers in the Department. Another 378 go overseas for the use of American ambassadors, Foreign Service officers, and representatives of the United States Information Agency. In addition, 157 copies of the *Monthly Survey* are distributed to officials in other government agencies in Washington and to the American delegation at the United Nations.

American Opinion Series Reports of from five to thirteen pages are issued weekly on the "Far East" and on "Germany and Related Issues," monthly on "American Private Organizations and Groups" and on the "United Nations," and quarterly on "Relations with Latin America." Between 130 and 260 copies of each publication are prepared, with two-thirds to three-fourths of the number going overseas to Foreign Service posts and to USIA representatives. Copies are also distributed, frequently through public affairs advisers in the appropriate geographic or functional bureaus, to interested Department officials and other government agencies.

The Staff furnishes one other useful summary on a regular basis for limited distribution. Twice a week, American opinion developments of the past half-week are summarized in a page or less for the Assistant Secretary for Public Affairs and his Deputy Assistant Secretary. Copies also go to leading White House advisers.

In addition to its regularly scheduled summaries, the Staff prepares special reports, perhaps on an area which becomes of particular importance, such as the Near East; on an economic question, such as foreign aid or East-West trade; or on the results of a public opinion poll.

An individualized service is often performed by the Staff when the Secretary of State attends a conference abroad. Special opinion summaries on a daily basis are forwarded to the Assistant Secretary for Public Affairs, who normally accompanies the Secretary to a conference. These summaries are fuller than the regular *Daily Opinion Summary* and include a condensation of major press stories as well as editorial comment on the conference. Such summaries were provided for the use of the Secretary at both London conferences on Suez. The Staff also forwards another special type of summary to the Secretary when he returns from a vacation, where he may have been more or less isolated from world affairs for a brief period. This summary provides a digest of opinion during his absence on foreign affairs topics.

Conclusions

Emphasis in this chapter upon the possible influence of public opinion at a variety of levels in the formulation and conduct of foreign policy should not obscure the fact that many other factors must be considered by the officials concerned. Harsh realities of balance of power in an imperfectly organized world cannot be ignored. Foreign governments have interests and opinions which must be carefully weighed. Information is available to Department officers which for security or diplomatic reasons cannot be widely distributed to Congress, the press, private organizations, or the general public. It would not be surprising, then, if foreign policy were frequently out of line with the opinion of these different publics. That this does not occur in greater degree or more often may demonstrate that foreign policy is formulated and implemented with an eye to whatever is possible on both the international and domestic scenes.

There are necessary lags of opinion which for a time tend to separate the Department from the Congress, the press, organized groups, and the general public, but over a period of time policy is the product of a mutual process of education and accommoda-

tion between the Department and its various publics. Enough of
the facts can be presented to Congress, the press, interested
groups, and John Q. Public to achieve a useful concurrence if a
policy is fundamentally sound. Knowledge of the opinions held
by individual publics, on the other hand, may help the Department reassess the validity of a policy.

Public opinion specialists are more interested in what ordinary
citizens think for determining broad limits of policy than for
obtaining new ideas to guide policy-makers. They are more interested in reactions to present policies than in suggestions for
new ones. The *Daily Opinion Summary,* as well as the weekly,
monthly, and area summaries, are valuable tools of the executive
branch for comprehending the broad public mind. They can
hardly be considered channels through which broad forward-looking ideas might cause redirection of foreign policy assumptions
and goals.

The work of the public opinion analysts in the Public Opinion
Studies Staff does contribute to a democratic exchange of opinion.
It makes public participation in the formulation of foreign policy
a limited reality. The development of some agreement on the
fundamentals of policy between the Department, Congress, private organizations, the press, and the general public lends
strength to the policy so conceived. The continuation of this
process of education and accommodation is in the best interests
of the United States and constitutes a living act of faith in the
democratic way of life.

Part Four

IS IT ENOUGH?

8 Survival Factor
A Fourth Dimension in Policy-Making?

THE THREE-DIMENSIONAL POLICY MACHINE

Detail is often deadly, but sometimes it makes perception possible. If dissection by careful description of six important parts in the Department of State mechanism has been tedious, the plunge down the rabbit hole into the wonderland of policy-making may yet provide a useful foundation for broader analysis of the policy machine. Many men—from stentorian Senator to poor old John Q. Public, who mostly listens, pays the bills, and has his pulse taken—have delusions of expertise when it comes to questions of American foreign policy and what is wrong with the State Department. Brass-rail diplomats are a dime a dozen, but most of them would long since have perished from mental indigestion had they swallowed all the facts set down here. Possessing no magic hat from which to pull easy solutions, and aware of the danger of facile but irresponsible recommendations, the more serious student of the policy machine embarks with trepidation upon even a tentative assessment of the policy-making mechanism as it is related to the search for survival in an evolving world situation.

No nation, whatever the splendor of its past, is guaranteed continued greatness. Although static thinking about dynamic problems can impair the national strength and hasten the descent from power, it is possible that no sacrifice, no adaptation to new conditions, however intelligent, will be sufficient for America to maintain its present role of international leadership. The development of new energy resources for industrial production, burgeoning populations in both densely and sparsely settled areas, economic progress and intellectual awakening in less developed lands, virtual revolutions in weapons systems, dramatic gains in transportation and communication, and the emergence or obsolescence of ideologies which fire the imaginations of men, can alter power relationships, can raise a nation up to or cast it down from a position of pre-eminence in world affairs. Measured against these gigantic forces, the role of the policy machine as an influence upon the course of history dwindles to relative insignificance. No one can project with certainty what the future holds in store for America or any other nation. We live in a period of transition and confusion made to order for twentieth century Cassandras; the heavens (cluttered by sputniks and luniks) resound with threats and florid congressional rhetoric.

The future for America is not so bleak as some would paint it, for all nations are affected by the moving forces of our time. Statesmen throughout the world, whatever their pontifical pronouncements and moral assurance, are forced to make decisions in relative darkness while retooling their thinking and adapting the principles of their craft to traumatic developments. They are all confronted by dangerous alternatives, bewildered by the shadowy imperatives—yet dimly perceived—of the hydrogen and rocket age. This is the time to keep our wits about us. If we use what we now know and what we can know in time to avert disaster, a bright tomorrow may still be possible. If one man has been trampled to death by a herd of wild horses, another has tamed the herd and learned to work with it to till the fields. Men have survived in the past by combining practical experience and theoretical knowledge to conquer what must have seemed overwhelming odds.

In a very real sense, the policy machine is a complex brain, the collective mind of our nation, which must remember enough of the past and learn enough about adjusting to the future to enable us to make the best possible adaptation to an onrushing tide of events which cannot be held back. The policy machine could be decisive in determining the destiny of America and Western civilization. If this be so, searching analysis and sincere efforts to improve it become of the utmost importance. Even if the machine were thought to have been perfect in the past (and few have claimed this), it would have to be carefully re-evaluated if we are to hope that it can meet the greater challenge of the future. We must ask ourselves if the policy machine is the best we can afford to build (but be aware that sheer expenditure is no measure of efficiency). To settle for anything less is to court catastrophe.

Over the past twelve years, at the peak of our national power, when world leadership and responsibility have been thrust upon America as never before and—perhaps—never again, we have toiled diligently in the international vineyards and reaped indifferent rewards. What can we expect to reap as others rise upward to join us on the high plateaus of world diplomacy, and compete with us more successfully for a place in the sun? Under such pressure, will we discover there is a survival factor missing in the policy-making process? Will we find that some structure or method of analysis is lacking in the policy machine which might assure America of a more peaceful and prosperous future, of continued influential participation in shaping the course of world events? If this be the case, what will it be? If found, could it recover for American decision-makers flexibility and room for maneuver on foreign policy questions, give reasonable promise of maintaining national security, provide the means by which America may use its leadership to reduce international tensions, gradually produce more rational responses to crisis situations, guide relations between states toward democratic processes, and result in a world more nearly at peace with itself? There can be no definite answers to such questions, but they are worthy of consideration.

The possibility that such a survival factor is to be found in Congress or among the general public is open to question, without rejecting the value of their roles in policy-making. The relationship of Congress and the public to the formulation of policy is of real importance; efforts need to be made to improve the methods and channels by which each makes its special con-

tributions.[1] Neither group is organized today, nor could easily
be organized, in such a way as to be able to project sustained
initiative in the international field, pay constant attention to
foreign policy questions, or contribute integrated and balanced
directives to the policy machine. Individual committees of Congress will contribute useful studies, drafted by consultants. Single
members will display flashes of insight and depth of perception
in speeches, often drafted by staff assistants. Private individuals
may do likewise although there are few George Kennans. University or other research centers, such as The Brookings Institution, may make profound contributions. But both the Congress
and the public, except on rare occasions and by a gifted few,
will devote most of their energies to serving as a check and review
on policies developed by the executive policy machine.

Of necessity, much of the initiative and continuing leadership
must come from the President and his advisers in the executive
branch of the government. The survival factor is likely to be found
here, if at all. Accepting this assumption as the basis for analysis,
a pause to review the structure of the executive policy complex is
in order.

Standing on the crest of Policy Hill in the executive branch
is the President, with umpteen other things on his mind, assisted
by the National Security Council and its subsidiary organs. The
purpose of the policy-making machine is to project, through
intelligence estimates, what situations may be in two, five, or
even ten years; to formulate broad policy goals to guide operations within such a period; and to develop specific implementations for achieving these goals.

There are three basic elements—three dimensions, if you will
—in the operation of the President's policy machine. Each makes
a valuable contribution to the effectiveness of American foreign
policy.

Just below the President and the National Security Council,
which is itself an interagency group (upon which the Secretary
represents the Department of State), are these basic elements in

[1] See Chapters Five and Seven.

the operation of the policy machine. They are three interagency bodies, each responsible in great measure for one dimension of the policy-making operation: (1) the United States Intelligence Board (the Director of Intelligence and Research represents State), which gives final approval to intelligence estimates evolved through the Central Intelligence Agency by the members of the intelligence community; (2) the National Security Council Planning Board (the Assistant Secretary for Policy Planning represents State), which makes a final check on integrated policy recommendations coming before the NSC from the departments or agencies; and (3) the Operations Coordinating Board (the Under Secretary for Political Affairs now represents State), which supervises through the cooperating departments and agencies the development of specific implementations for broad NSC policies and reports back to the NSC on field operations.

Within the Department of State, intelligence estimates which will be blended into the final draft approved by the United States Intelligence Board are originally prepared by intelligence analysts in the Bureau of Intelligence and Research. The broad policy papers which will be incorporated into the draft accepted by the National Security Council Planning Board have been monitored by the Policy Planning Staff, and sometimes drafted by country desk officers with the assistance of intelligence analysts. The implementation plans and operations reports which will be screened through board assistants to the Operations Coordinating Board often have been drafted originally by country desk officers in the Department's regional bureaus, serving as members of interagency working groups.

From this brief review, the policy machine appears to be a well-organized mechanism. But, is it enough? Is there a missing dimension?

THE NEED FOR A FOURTH DIMENSION

In 1947, Secretary of State George Marshall and President Harry Truman took a "calculated risk," the Marshall Plan. It bolstered Europe's tattered economic resources, restored economic viability, made possible some degree of military strength, and produced enlightened steps toward European unity which have culminated (for the time being) in the agreement for a common market. Practical necessity plus knowledge drawn from economics and applied through knowledge of political science brought this program to a successful conclusion, created in Europe a force capable of resisting the expansive pressures of communism directed by the Soviet Union, then probing an area of weakness in an attempt to alter the world balance of power. The Marshall Plan was one implementation of a "containment" policy. The rationale or justification for such a policy had first appeared in despatches written by George Kennan from Moscow in 1946. Later, speaking as a leading State Department authority on the Soviet Union and Director of the newly created Policy Planning Staff, Kennan presented his ideas as a lecture at the National War College. Finally, his conclusions were made public in the now famous Mr. X article, "The Sources of Soviet Conduct," *Foreign Affairs,* July, 1947.

In 1949 (according to Department experts), Secretary of State Dean Acheson, perhaps without consulting President Truman, rejected a second "calculated risk." In a preparatory paper (which would be most interesting to read) for the Council of Foreign Ministers' meeting held in Paris during late May and June, 1949, Kennan—after two years as Director of the Policy Planning Staff —offered a tentative plan for resolving the German problem. In essence, it is said to be based on assumptions similar to those implicit in his six Reith Lectures on "Russia, the Atom, and the West" in the fall of 1957 over the facilities of the British Broadcasting Corporation. Kennan apparently assumed that the Soviet Union was not immutably intent on armed conquest of Western Europe, that a carefully phased disengagement might pave the way for German reunification and reduce East-West tensions. (A member of the Policy Planning Staff who served under Kennan recently observed, "The only startling thing about Kennan's 1957 proposals was their familiarity. He was projecting ideas like these in our staff discussions in 1949.") He was overruled. Tensions and rearmament reached new highs. Germany remained divided. America suffered through the Korean police action. Although Kennan must have believed greater flexibility was possible in American policy toward the Soviet Union as early as 1949 (long before Stalin's death in 1953), his own inflexible policy of containment—enunciated two years earlier—remained the guiding star of American policy-makers for almost a decade. How seriously were the fundamental assumptions upon which this policy is based ever questioned? How often?

In the period since the BBC lectures, Kennan's 1949 thesis has arisen once more to plague the policy-makers, to demand consideration as an alternative to containment. The challenge has been generated not from within the policy machine but from without, from Kennan's position as a private citizen extraordinary. It is impossible to rewrite history, but it is interesting to speculate what differences there might now be in Soviet-American relations —what events might not have occurred—had Kennan's plan been accepted as the American position at Paris in 1949. On the other hand, who can say that Secretary Acheson was not right? Even if some distortion has crept into this casual retelling of what may have been a critical moment of choice in the direction of American foreign policy, it serves to emphasize the difficulty of decision-making and the importance of constructive ideas.

There should be no question of the Secretary of State's right to rule against a recommendation by his top policy-planner. The point is that new ideas, challenging the basic assumptions as well as the goals and implementations of policy, should be pumped regularly into the policy machine for consideration by the Secretary and the President. As Secretary Acheson said on April 25, 1949, testifying on the role of the Policy Planning Staff before the House Committee on Foreign Affairs, "There are many plans which were formulated and on which the operating people are going ahead. With the passage of time, such plans become no longer useful. However, an operating fellow is not likely to see that. He just drives in every morning at quarter to nine and carries on policy. He may seem to be getting into hot water, but that just calls for more courage and determination. Mr. Kennan is sitting back there and says, 'This thing is outmoded. We shouldn't be doing this anymore. This is a waste of time. Do it differently, or scrap it, or change the whole thing.' He is both forewarner and foreplanner on problems, and he is the critic. He says: 'What we are doing was fine when we started, but it is no longer a proper answer to the thing we are dealing with.'"

Recalling the workload of the desk officer in the Department of State's regional bureaus, Secretary Acheson's comment on the "operating fellow" seems eminently correct. "He just drives in . . . and carries on policy." At the desk officer and office director level in policy-making, decisions are made within an agreed frame of reference, often a country or regional policy paper approved by the President after consideration by the National Security Council and—even more specific—an Operations Coordinating Board paper on implementation. Also restrictive in effect is the hierarchal nature of the policy-making structure. Each officer on the policy ladder looks up to see where the one above is going, what he thinks. Too many differences of opinion are likely to destroy the policy-maker's usefulness to his superiors, require too much of their time in review, consume too much of their energy in redrafting his statements. Ideas must be consistent with the assumptions, goals, and implementations which have been accepted by his Assistant Secretary, the Secretary, and the President. If intelligence reports indicate conditions developing abroad which require adjustments in policy, the changes considered must not conflict with a host of other policies already in operation. Most papers reaching the top decision-makers, even if a difference remains to be resolved, pose alternatives within the approved framework. At the lower and middle level in policy-making, there seems to be little room left for flexibility.

Flexibility, implied Secretary Acheson, is maintained by the Policy Planning Staff. His assessment of the role of the staff was realistic in 1949. (This was the year of Kennan's recommendation for "disengagement" as a means of resolving the German problem.) Kennan was saying, "What we are doing was fine when we started, but it is no longer a proper answer to the thing we are dealing with." It was still possible at that time for a member of the staff to question the fundamental assumptions upon which American foreign policy was based. The function of the Policy Planning Staff, through no fault of its own, seems to have become somewhat more limited by 1960. The change has occurred so gradually that members of the staff may hardly be aware of it themselves. Certainly, they do not admit it publicly. Some of their time is now taken up in feeding the hungry maw of the National Security Council structure, in reviewing policy papers or monitoring revisions of existing policy papers, and in backstopping preparation of the Secretary of State for National Security Council meetings. What they help funnel into the NSC complex, for the sake of practicality, must present alternatives consistent with the main body of thought already existing in more than forty-two NSC policy papers which have been approved by the President. Even in considering what are essentially Department problems, the Policy Planning Staff must work within the general framework of assumptions, goals, and implementations which have been accepted by the President, the National Security Council, and the Operations Coordinating Board. A member of the Policy Planning Staff can say with great truthfulness, "There is really very little room for maneuver on foreign policy questions." Of course, many of the limitations upon American initiative in policy-making stem from forces outside the control of the policy machine—from the Soviet bloc, our allies, the neutrals, Congress, public opinion, limited national resources, conflicts between departments or agencies of government, or even differences between bureaus within the Department of State. But, one can wonder if much of the inflexibility—and the most critical portion of it—is not self-imposed, resulting from the very structure of the policy machine and the growing mass of policy which it has ground out over the past thirteen years.

The highly competitive, inter-departmental nature of the NSC structure has made Department of State policy-makers wary of its processes, and has led them to question its usefulness for dealing with critical problems. *Ad hoc* solutions are now sought outside the structure if at all possible. State hesitates to take any new question within the NSC machinery, finding it difficult enough to wrestle with revision of those problems already mired in the swamp of inter-agency double talk. Misuse of the NSC structure is likely to grow if means are not found for channeling new ideas to all participating agencies, both to give them a greater degree of common understanding of foreign policy problems and to get them off the dime which thirteen long years of NSC policy-building has left them standing on.

Consistency is a virtue until it demands conformity; then it becomes a vice. The policy-makers at all levels, limited in maneuverability and in the flexibility of their thinking, become technicians, and are prevented from reconsidering basic assumptions. They can tinker and repair, but they cannot rebuild from scratch. They attempt to face an ever-changing climate and environment of international relations in pretty much the same old way, perhaps not oblivious to but unable to confront alternative assumptions, concerning the nature of man and the world we live in, which challenge the whole policy structure they have so patiently constructed. They can change the routine, but it is still vaudeville in a world where the more exacting techniques of television reign supreme.

If in earlier days the opinion of experts outside government was often solicited by the Policy Planning Staff, more recently most of the men called in for consultation seem to be either American ambassadors, former directors of the staff, or high officials from other government departments and agencies. Certainly ideas from these practical sources (excluding Kennan) are likely to yield suggestions which may be suitable alternatives within the accepted policy framework. Whether they provide (except for Kennan) brave new ideas is open to question. Members of today's Policy Planning Staff, after being presented with facts and after consulting with experts, tend to agree on solutions to problems, although they are encouraged to be critical, probably because they have acquired a common pattern of thought, and reason within the same framework. Four of the ten Staff-members in April 1959 were Foreign Service officers, with regional specialities or general knowledge of several areas. Another four had rather long experience in the Department or other government agencies. Three of these men possess backgrounds in functional specialties, i.e., intelligence, the United Nations, law and atomic energy. A fourth is a regional specialist. The two remaining members of the Staff have entered government service more recently. One is an economist. The other, a former Ambassador to Ireland, is becoming an African specialist. The Staff is more than adequate for the function it presently performs, but it seems like a terribly practical group which might require several "Kennan types" to enliven discussions.

This analysis implies no criticism of the present role of the Policy Planning Staff nor of its members. It is performing a necessary but limited function. So far as one can determine, its members are all very able men. It is extremely doubtful that it would have been possible by any means, in view of the rise of the National Security Council system, for the Policy Planning Staff to continue to perform completely the original function outlined for it by Secretary Acheson. Acceptance of the present role of the Policy Planning Staff does not imply that the policy machine can continue successful operations for long without finding some means of restoring the lost function. What is now missing from the policy machine is an appendage which could provide seminal ideas and a continuing challenge to the basic assumptions, goals, and implementations of American foreign policy. This is the missing fourth dimension, the part of the machine most necessary to provide the survival factor during the years of fluidity and change through which the world is now passing.

RESEARCH FOR SURVIVAL

Although problems are easier found than solutions, to pose a problem invites solution. If there is a need for a flow of ideas and a continuing challenge to the policies manufactured by the machine, there may be several methods by which such a survival factor might be introduced into the policy-making process. The real problem is to discover possible sources of such ideas, means of stimulating and developing better ideas, and a way of channeling these ideas to the policy-makers.[2] This may sound simple, but it is a difficult problem and involves complex considerations.

The concept of providing fresh insights to policy-makers and diplomats is not new. Eleanor Roosevelt, in her disarming fashion, used to say that she often wished a psychologist were sitting behind her during negotiations at the United Nations. He could help her understand the responses of those with whom she was dealing and remind her if her own reasoning became emotional or non-rational. James Reston, writing in the *New York Times,* has noted the contributions of individual scholars (like Kennan) in proposing solutions to foreign policy questions and wondered if even more could not be accomplished if men of stature could be brought together to work in groups.

Within the Department of State, policy-makers are confronted daily with ideas from outside the machine. Most policy-makers read the *New York Times,* possibly several other papers as well. Periodicals circulated by the Library Division of the Office of Intelligence Resources and Coordination are in continuous motion through the Department. The men on the German political desk have read Acheson's *Power and Diplomacy* as well as Kennan's *Russia, the Atom and the West.* Personnel selected to attend the National War College or the new Senior Officer Course at the Foreign Service Institute are exposed to a variety of ideas from both private scholars and government experts. The members of the Policy Planning Staff on occasion still consult with private individuals; Congressmen sometimes drop in at the Department of State and can express their views. Some few letters among the many from the general public contain useful ideas which

[2] For an interesting discussion of some aspects of this problem, see Henry A. Kissinger, "The Policymaker and the Intellectual," *The Reporter,* March 5, 1959, pp. 30–35.

reach the Department officers who formulate or approve replies.

There are more formal devices which have been used in the past or which are still used from time to time. In pre-McCarthy days, when the Department was less security-conscious, a number of professors were sometimes invited to participate in special group conferences with Department policy officers on major problems of American foreign policy.[3] In 1954, with more caution, the Secretary of State appointed a public committee on personnel, mentioned earlier, under the leadership of Henry M. Wriston which rendered yeoman service, brought together top Department officials and outstanding men from private life to give sustained consideration to personnel problems and to recommend integration of Department and Foreign Service personnel.

Unfortunately, the Department has never had funds for analyzing its own documents used in past negotiations as a means of learning what or what not to do in the future, but some other agencies of government have conducted such research, probably for the benefit of the agency position rather than for general improvement of American diplomacy. One formal device for keeping policy-makers abreast of current periodical material was dropped in the 1953 economy wave. Before that time, an analyst on what is now the Public Opinion Studies Staff of the Bureau of Public Affairs prepared weekly summaries of articles related to foreign policy in leading magazines. Although public opinion polls are less valuable in providing new ideas than in indicating the possible limits of policy-making, the loss of this service to the Department in 1957, with no current plans for restoration, may become an increasing problem. If funds are low and some Department sources of outside ideas have tended to dry up in recent years, the Senate Foreign Relations Committee, through its special subcommittees, has contracted for research by leading academic or other private institutions which has produced a wealth of information of great value to the Senate, occasionally considered useful within the Department as well. Much of the material in

---

[3] This practice has been reinstituted. Such a conference was held on Latin American foreign policy problems in February, 1959.

such studies may be gathered from Department officers by the private researchers. The contribution to the Department is a point of view rather than factual information.

This hodge-podge of uncoordinated material which is injected haphazardly into the stream of Department thinking must have some effect upon policy-making. From time to time, either inexplicably or backed by sufficient congressional discontent, it brings the machine to a grinding halt and starts it off in a new direction, although still consistent with the great body of National Security Council policy. But it would appear to be a most inefficient means of searching for survival, and one might fear that the machine would sometimes go into the ditch before the drivers became aware of the information which might have led them to make the turn at the right time. Even if one were to believe that present knowledge of human behavior, in both its domestic and international aspects, is sufficient to resolve the crushing problems of our time (and this is probably not so), the lack of integration of such information as it flows uncertainly into the parts and pieces of the policy machine usually results in an impact about equal to the bite of one small fly upon the most insensitive portion of one large elephant. How can a single challenging idea, no matter how well argued, be more than modestly effective against the mountain of consistent detail intricately blended into the approved body of National Security Council policy? If one realizes, in addition, that we have embarked upon programs in the physical sciences which threaten to alter man's basic social relationships beyond recognition—and remembers the social lag present even in more stable societies of yesteryear—the scope of our problem looms even larger.

The government is pouring millions of dollars into theoretical research in the physical sciences and billions into the application of such research findings to practical projects, i.e., Vanguard, Thor, Polaris, Jupiter. Research and experimentation in the physical sciences are recognized as ways to win the cold war, to preserve peace in our time, to maintain American security. There is missing from the government and among its leaders any comparable recognition of the value of theoretical and applied research in the social and behavioral fields as related to the formulation and conduct of American foreign policy. There is no encouragement from high sources for this type of research—in psychology, sociology, anthropology, economics, political science, even semantics and group dynamics—so that America can better learn how to control the weapons of destruction which we assume will help us preserve the peace, but which will also prove useful for war. Nowhere in the Department of State nor in the National Security Council structure is there an attempt made either to stimulate social research or to bring its findings to bear directly in any integrated way upon the formulation and conduct of American foreign policy. Social and behavioral knowledge can perhaps contribute more to American destiny than a moderately intelligent citizenry, practicing law or journalism, or working in store and factory. There may be a creative role for the social disciplines, illuminated on rare occasions by great teachers, carried on more rarely still by scholars devoted to research. Modern social and behavioral research functions in no ivory tower of impracticability; it employs many of the methodological techniques of mathematics and the physical sciences. If America is to survive the changes to be wrought in the world by developments in the physical sciences, if American democracy is to be adapted and defended in parlous times of social readjustment, the President may find it necessary to develop a program for the stimulation of theoretical and applied research on social and behavioral problems. He may need to authorize application in limited areas and to limited functional problems of foreign policy some of the best tentative working hypotheses which the researchers can evolve. Even those aware of the present inadequacy of knowledge in social and behavioral fields may be hard pressed to suggest a more practical source and method for hammering out a realistic American adaptation to a rapidly changing world scene.

In a world hurtling toward either destruction or salvation—or struggling endlessly in a morass of confusion—America will do well to draw on its best resources, in social disciplines as well as physical, and look to the far reaches of the various subject-matter fields, to the men in the forefront of the search for knowledge. Their ideas could be channeled to specialists in the fields of international relations, foreign policy, and government employed within the policy machine. These specialists (possessing both academic and government experience) could discuss, integrate, and supervise the experimental application of the basic principles of social and behavioral knowledge in a forward-looking way from within the National Security Council framework. They could search for ideas from any source which would enable them to recommend to the President and lower-level policy-makers the "calculated risks" worth taking—in the light of all knowledge available—to preserve an American way of life and assure useful participation of America as a partner among nations in the centuries to come.

Taken by itself, a single fresh insight in one social field may seem useless and insignificant. Properly interpreted, synthesized with the total body of knowledge and principles which the social and behavioral disciplines might be able to draw together, it may provide the spark in a specific operational problem which would relate present decisions to future needs. This process might yield to the American policy-makers an exciting new dimension for comprehending the scope of the problems confronting them, depth of perception and extended vision of the future, insights never before achieved by men. Mankind has yet to attain the ultimate organization for realization of its heartfelt goals. We cry for peace, but there is no peace; it does not come for the asking. Our foreign policy actions seem to contain within themselves the seeds of their own failure, and encourage development of counter-vailing forces which deny them the possibility of success. If this calamitous paradox is to be resolved, it will be through research and more research, integration of principles and reintegration, experiment in limited areas and more experiment. There is no royal road to the social knowledge which can bring peace, prosperity, and democracy to nations in their relations with each other. And it should be recognized that no matter what our efforts, we are likely to fall short of complete attainment of these "perfectionist" ideals.

THE EXISTING CORE OF KNOWLEDGE

There is already a great core of knowledge existing in the social and behavioral fields which further research could refine, which experimentation could test in practical situations. As examples of the principles in this core of knowledge—as isolated illustrations only—let us focus on practical ideas from each of three disciplines: political science, psychology, and group dynamics.

Political science, the oldest of the three, is sometimes viewed as sterile and descriptive; psychology is attaining some degree of maturity and is even being applied in major political campaigns; group dynamics is a relative newcomer but has already produced some provocative ideas.

Political scientists have long discussed the relationship between the establishment of a balance of power or equilibrium between states and maintenance of peaceful conditions. Emmerich de Vattel, in his work *The Law of Nations*, first published in 1758, confessed: "Confederations would be a sure means of preserving the balance of power and thus maintaining the liberty of Nations, if all sovereigns were constantly aware of their true interests, and if they regulated their policy according to the welfare of the State. But powerful sovereigns succeed only too often in winning for themselves partisans and allies who are blindly devoted to their designs. Dazzled by the glitter of present advantage, seduced by their greed, deceived by unfaithful ministers, how many princes become the instruments of power which will one day swallow up either themselves or their successors." There remains enough of truth in this sage observation to explain the desire of many states to remain neutral in the cold war which has disturbed international relations since World War II. Repeated expressions of good intentions and the use of pressure to encourage the joining of power blocs are not going to affect favorably the national leaders whose countries have only recently achieved independence from British, French, or Dutch imperialism.

Once a balance of power is established, it is almost axiomatic that war is preferable to peace whenever a great power is threatened by an unfavorable breakdown of the balance. Is this still true? If it is, states would do well to attempt to create stable but flexible equilibriums with some hope that they will not go rapidly out of balance, and can be adjusted to variables which may tend to destroy the balance. When a balance of power is multi-polar in nature, involving a large number of states, each possessing a moderate degree of strength, each interested in preserving its own security, each willing under certain circumstances to shift its position in the balance for the sake of maintaining the equilibrium, a stable balance of power exists. If one state or complex power unit becomes aggressive and seeks to gain increasing power, other states or complex power units combine against this threat to their security. When the number of states or power units in balance is small, when there is considerable disparity in the strength of states within the power unit, and when states are bound by permanent alliances or rigid neutrality obligations, the degree of stability is low. As a rule, there are few states available to shift position, and these are unlikely to do so because of lack of strength, because of alliances or because of rigid neutrality. Both the bi-polar nature of the Soviet-American balance of power and recent centrifugal tendencies within each side of the equilibrium are significant to the political scientist. It leads him to view George Kennan's proposals for disengagement with more than passing interest. The eventual rise of a third power bloc or the presence of additional uncommitted states would be helpful to the preservation of world peace, and might buy time for other developments leading toward a more rational relationship between the great powers.

The psychologist in viewing the current world scene might point out that even declared intent of world conquest need not be taken at face value or as an immutable pattern if conditions change. He could cite numerous instances where individuals undergoing treatment have threatened actions because of insecurity (or other reasons) which they did not wish to carry out; indeed, will not, if the proper response is forthcoming. In studying post-World War II history, he might say that it is almost impossible to determine the motivation which a state may have for carrying out some specific act, yet it was the practice of opposing states to make assumptions as to what the motivation was and to take action accordingly. Soviet-American diplomats early developed as their basic assumption the belief that each others' state was intent upon and could not be deflected from world domination except by the exertion of counter-force (by political, military, economic, or propaganda means). As a result, each act of the "enemy" has been interpreted as a step, either devious or direct, toward such an end. Each state, therefore, feels it necessary to retaliate by some measure which will prevent the accomplishment of this end. Such "defensive" measures appear "offensive" to the opponent. As a result, counter-measures must be taken against these new "aggressive" acts. This process, a series of over-reactions with a resultant spiral of tension, leads to what may be called the mutual validation of expectation. Each state accuses the other of aggressive designs and, therefore, acts in a way which encourages the opponent to carry out over-reactive measures which are seen as further proof of aggressive intent. The defense of South Korea and the elimination of the aggressor south of the Thirty-eighth Parallel is considered a legitimate reaction; the subsequent crossing of the parallel and the invasion of North Korea, an over-reaction.

The policy which the psychologist might advocate here is not one of appeasement. Rather, it is one of reason and firmness, of proving by pushing the aggressor back to his original position that change of the status quo cannot be achieved by force. It would be suggested that "punishment" (invasion) for such an outbreak or a harsh verbal attack (name-calling and scapegoating) tend to be unsound psychologically if the hope is eventually to build more friendly relations between nations. Reaction to defend the collective security is advocated. Over-reaction seems both unnecessary and unwise. The advance of United Nations troops north of the Thirty-eighth Parallel helped place a Republican President in the White House in the American national election of 1952. It changed a successful campaign to repel an aggressor into a dubious conflict with the rising power on the Asian mainland. It so affected American public opinion toward the Chinese Communist regime that American policy in the Far East today can only be compared to that of an ostrich sticking its head in the sand. The Chinese Communists may no longer care whether we recognize them or not.

Students of group dynamics and non-directive counseling might have interesting suggestions on the exchange of notes and visits of foreign ministers or heads of state which may or may not lead to further summit conferences. Group dynamics, in brief, is the study of how groups function within themselves and in relationship both to other groups and individuals. In non-directive counseling, the counselor refrains from giving advice or interpretations but listens so sympathetically that the person being counseled gains insight into his problems through his own efforts to formulate them. He utters his beliefs more freely than if he were under public criticism. His ideas are being "accepted" and "understood." He is freed at this point, for the first time, to examine his attitudes instead of just having them or defending them. He can begin to ask why he believes what he does, to re-evaluate his attitudes. His problems, seen in the light of his re-evaluation, may no longer remain in the form originally conceived. Having become more rational in discerning what the problems are, he may now attempt a new and more objective solution.

The study of group dynamics in relation to the problem of tension between nations might demonstrate that most negotiations are carried on at a level intended for public consumption. The negotiators may not even realize that the arguments used are only rationalizations and that the problems raised are not those which actually separate them. Only under conditions where discussions move from a public to a private level of motivation, where the diplomats are able to understand and to explain what is really disturbing their nations, will actual problems stand revealed. Only then can rational solutions to problems be sought. Non-directive counseling techniques may be useful in making such conditions possible in summit negotiations between the East and West. It may be true that diplomats of both countries spend too much time arguing at a public level of motivation about problems which are not basic, ignoring the real causes of their separation. This situation is prolonged under conditions where no sympathetic listener is present. Each state's negotiator wants to point out to his counterpart where the other's state is wrong. Each is so busy defending the position of his government that no chance exists to evaluate or change the position of his government. By actually listening to what the other representative has to say and by assisting him to say it more clearly, it may be possible to conduct useful discussions leading toward an easing of world tensions.

Researchers in the field of group dynamics and non-directive counseling might agree with James Reston's puckish suggestion in the *New York Times:*

"The objection to a free-for-all foreign ministers' meeting is that reporters might be all over the place, gleefully hurling blow-by-blow descriptions of every tussle into the press of a baffled world.

"Franklin D. Roosevelt had an answer to this problem. He did his skirmishing on boats, preferably battleships, on the high seas, with the reporters tossing and cursing on destroyers just beyond the horizon. It is a wicked thought, but in a pinch, it might be revived."

The sample principles from three disciplines do not provide a real understanding of the new dimension of thinking which the social and behavioral disciplines could add to the policy-making process. They are isolated generalizations and have not been correlated and evaluated within the totality of specific knowledge accepted as working hypotheses by social and behavioral researchers. Their significance lies only in calling attention to the fact that in each instance the general principle illustrated has been largely ignored in the formulation and conduct of American foreign policy in the post-World War II era. We sought to build a rigid alliance system and continue to fight against developing flexibility in the bi-polar balance of power. We sent our troops across the Thirty-eighth Parallel in Korea to our great regret. We continue to over-react, verbally and physically, and thus justify in many neutral eyes Soviet responses to our policies. We have talked of negotiations; we have hurled charges and counter-charges (sometimes because we were not ready to reach agreement), but we have yet to engage in serious, quiet conversations where a full exploration could be made, without a running account in the press, of the real problems which separate the East and West. As a matter of fact, we may negotiate on the basis of documents which are Don Quixotic in quality, leading us to contend over factors which are not actually essential to the achievement of modest agreement.

Men trained in the social and behavioral fields are present at many levels in the three-dimensional policy mechanism. Material written by scholars and researchers is not completely ignored in their calculations. There is undoubtedly some reflection on the conditions of the balance of power, upon the possibility of over-reaction, upon the best methods to pursue in negotiation. The point made here is that such consideration is isolated in nature, is more a happenstance recollection of principle than a studied application, often if vaguely recalled is thrown out because short-term necessity is served first in short-range planning. Present social knowledge has not been collected, selectively organized, integrated, and mobilized to work for the long-range interests of the United States. The principles relevant to foreign policy have not been selected out of their individual disciplines and considered as a body of knowledge. It is this new discipline, the whole of which is more than the sum of its parts, which must be brought to serve America. The problem is to integrate new research from the older social studies into an emergent discipline of international relations (with emphasis upon the formulation and conduct of foreign policy), applying its conclusions to the making of foreign policy for the purpose of achieving America's long-range goals.

Country desk officers and their betters in the Department have had some exposure to the social studies in their college years. In-service training has provided more, but much of the emphasis has been on the study of areas concerning which we were grievously lacking in knowledge. There is an Office of Functional and Biographic Intelligence which includes a small external research staff, but its interest lies overseas rather than in the general or specific principles of human relations which might be useful in the making or carrying out of foreign policy. Studies by the Historical Office present some perspective but are devoid of real social and behavioral analysis. There are sometimes historians and economists on the Policy Planning Staff, but even here the emphasis is on regional specialty in most instances. This is normal in view of the Department's past practice of conducting policy formulation and operations primarily through the regional bureaus. This recitation demonstrates only too clearly that the Department as presently organized has no effective mechanism for channeling social and behavioral information to the policy-makers.

THE SURVIVAL FACTOR?

A critical question remains. What sort of reconstruction of the policy machine will restore the flow of ideas and provide a continuing challenge to the basic assumptions, goals, and implementations of American foreign policy? The problem is to design a structure adequate to perform the missing function. How do we install the survival factor? Should some new part be appended to the present machine? Can a fourth dimension be blended into the policy-making complex without duplicating or affecting adversely the functions already being effectively performed in the present three-dimensional machine? If we take a "calculated risk" and spell out a tentative design, what guide lines shall we follow? What difficulties can we foresee and forestall?

The new structure should be simple and fit into and complement the present complex policy machine. Additional paper work and personnel should be held to a minimum. If ideas are to be injected at all levels of policy-making, and this seems essential, the structure must parallel in some measure the hierarchal nature of the machine now in operation. A systematic, staggered rotation of personnel may be necessary. This might assist the new mechanism to attain sufficient practicality to adapt fresh insights to the needs of the over-all policy machine. No matter how carefully personnel are selected, the development of satisfactory relationships with other parts of the machine will require patience, tact, and responsible leadership. Men will make or break the evolving effectiveness of the new mechanism. Obviously, there are many methods for injecting ideas into the existing policy machine; undoubtedly, most present formal and informal devices should be continued. There is probably no one right or perfect structure which can be improvised, but let us construct and consider a model which appears practical. This particular plan may be neither important nor the best that can be designed, but the idea it represents is vital.

To incorporate the fourth dimension in policy-making, the establishment of a Social Research Board within the National Security Council structure is recommended. The Board would function at the level of the NSC Planning Board, the Operations Coordinating Board, and the United States Intelligence Board. Departments or agencies participating on the Social Research Board would be the Department of State, the Department of Defense, the International Cooperation Administration, the United States Information Agency, and the Central Intelligence Agency. Social Research Board reports and recommendations would be channeled to the National Security Council for consideration by NSC members and the President. (See Chart 2 for the major elements in the Executive Structure for the formulation of foreign policy, and for the relationship of the proposed Social Research Board.)

The following functions might be assigned to the Social Research Board by the National Security Council:

1. to collect, organize, and analyze ideas or recommendations

from any available source bearing on assumptions, goals, or implementations of American foreign policy;

2. to advise the National Security Council and the participating agencies of social and behavioral research developments related to all aspects of foreign policy;

3. to recommend areas or projects within the social or behavioral disciplines where special assistance might provide a break-through in research likely to have foreign policy applications;

4. to recommend possible application of principles of integrated social and behavioral research to normal short-range (two to ten years) policy-planning and to current operations;

5. to recommend possible application of principles of integrated social and behavioral research in assessing long-range assumptions, goals, and policies (looking ten or more years ahead);

6. to recommend special experiments in the application of social and behavioral research theories to current operations in restricted areas or to limited problems;

7. to maintain liaison with the Operations Coordinating Board to guide the conduct and to assess the results of such experimentation.

Joining the Special Assistants for National Security Affairs and for Security Operations Coordination and their staffs within the National Security Council structure would be a Special Assistant to the President for Social and Behavioral Research, with an appropriate staff. Within the participating agencies, special Social Research Planning Staffs would be created. They would each consist of ten members and a Director for Social Research Planning. He would be the representative to the Social Research Board.

One member selected from the Social Research Planning Staff in each department or agency would serve as a representative to a Social Research Board Assistants group which would help prepare materials for the consideration of the Social Research Board. Another member of the Planning Staff would be

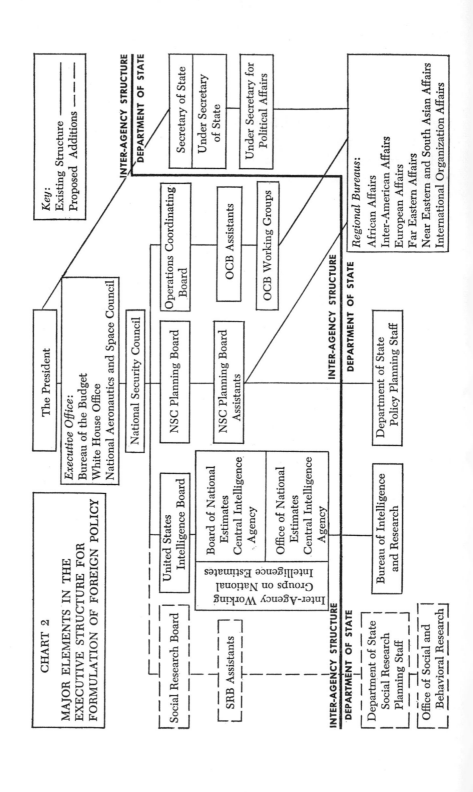

CHART 2

MAJOR ELEMENTS IN THE
EXECUTIVE STRUCTURE FOR
FORMULATION OF FOREIGN POLICY

Key:
Existing Structure ————
Proposed Additions ————

INTER-AGENCY STRUCTURE
DEPARTMENT OF STATE

The President

Executive Office:
Bureau of the Budget
White House Office
National Aeronautics and Space Council

National Security Council

Operations Coordinating Board

NSC Planning Board

OCB Assistants

NSC Planning Board Assistants

OCB Working Groups

Secretary of State

Under Secretary of State

Under Secretary for Political Affairs

Inter-Agency Working Groups on National Intelligence Estimates

United States Intelligence Board

Board of National Estimates
Central Intelligence Agency

Office of National Estimates
Central Intelligence Agency

Social Research Board

SRB Assistants

INTER-AGENCY STRUCTURE
DEPARTMENT OF STATE

Department of State
Social Research Planning Staff

Office of Social and Behavioral Research

Bureau of Intelligence and Research

Department of State
Policy Planning Staff

INTER-AGENCY STRUCTURE
DEPARTMENT OF STATE

Regional Bureaus:
African Affairs
Inter-American Affairs
European Affairs
Far Eastern Affairs
Near Eastern and South Asian Affairs
International Organization Affairs

assigned liaison duties with the present Policy Planning Staff in each agency; a third, liaison duties with the Operations Coordinating Board activities within the department or agency. Other members of the Social Research Planning Staff might each be expected to possess a competence in one of the social or behavioral disciplines and a general knowledge of government and foreign policy, and to develop an interest in some regional or functional problem. Representation should give coverage to the fields of political science, economics, history, geography, socio-anthropology, psychology, semantics, and group dynamics. One member might be a journalist to provide knowledge of and liaison with major national publications and publishers. Selection of members for Social Research Planning Staffs might be made by the secretary or director of appropriate departments or agencies from lists of scholars or journalists approved or recommended by recognized national professional organizations.

A staggered system of rotation would allow members of the Research Planning Staffs to serve an average of two years, providing both experience and a continuous flow of new ideas. Not the least advantage of drawing academic personnel into such an adventure in "practical ideas" would be the spread effect of such an experience as they returned to their institutions of learning and research across America. Their own research for ideas would be stimulated; they could communicate needs to researchers in special fields who might otherwise never be aware of the possible relationships of their work to the conduct of American foreign policy. Membership on a social research planning group should not preclude reappointment to the same or another group in the social research planning structure after further research or teaching experience.

As a backstop for the gathering of information and as a specialized channel to bring material to the attention of the Research Planning Staffs, a special Office of Social and Behavioral Research would be established within each participating department or agency (appended directly to its Research Planning Staff). The Office Director and a designated representative of the Bureau of

Intelligence and Research would participate in meetings of the Department of State's Research Planning Staff. As a coordinating device with the operating bureaus, a Social Research Planning Adviser could be attached to the staff of each Assistant Secretary of the five regional bureaus in the Department of the State. As an outside source of research, less fettered by bureaucratic considerations, and as a backstop to the social and behavioral research machinery which has been proposed within the NSC structure, it is further recommended that a Social and Behavioral Research Corporation be set up—possibly a Rand-type research body—to service all levels of the new mechanism.

Such an organization, in its totality, would allow the integration of social and behavioral research materials and their consideration at each level of policy-making in the Department of State and within the government-wide structure of the National Security Council. It would not allow the recommendations of the social research staff members at any level to outweigh other important policy considerations, but it would provide a fourth dimension in the formulation and conduct of foreign policy.

The cost of implementing such a proposal is infinitesimal by normal government standards. Americans are hardly likely to quibble over the cost of an organization if they believe it will provide the survival factor for an American way of life and Western civilization for centuries to come. The more serious question is whether they or their leaders will understand the real significance of this recommendation to themselves and to future generations or be able to agree on the form of its implementation.

It is quite possible that the survival of our way of life and a useful role for America in world affairs at the turn of the century depend in some measure on what we now know but do not fully comprehend and are not using. Survival may also depend on what we can learn if we show sufficient determination in stimulating imaginative social and behavioral research and have an efficient mechanism for applying its findings in farsighted fashion to the formulation and conduct of American foreign policy.

9 Personnel Management
Matching People and Jobs

REQUIREMENTS AND DILEMMAS

An essential ingredient in the future foreign policy mechanism, as in any organization, will be competent people. Because the international problems confronting the United States will be of crucial significance for the survival—and hopefully, the improvement—of the democratic way of life, the foreign policy process deserves a substantial proportion of the best talents available to the nation. At present it is apparent that the foreign policy function does not always compete successfully with the private employers in providing satisfying lifetime careers for first-class personnel. In part, this situation is merely a segment of the larger problem of strengthening the entire governmental service, particularly at the upper levels. In part, however, the foreign policy personnel question is unique.

The prospective developments in world affairs present a wide range of requirements for various kinds of people and skills. There are, however, certain general qualities that will be particularly valuable, especially among the leadership. As always, basic intelligence will be at a premium. Unassailable integrity will be essential to withstand the extraordinary moral strains that will arise. Persevering motivation to serve the public cause will be necessary to surmount disheartening trials. A sense of how to get large numbers of people to work together efficiently and in a democratic spirit will be necessary to achieve maximum gain with minimum expenditure of resources and energy. And a broad understanding of and sensitivity to the great political, economic, and social developments that are unfolding both at home and abroad will temper the motivation and enlighten the action.

If persons responsible for formulating personnel policies are in basic agreement on the desirability of implementing these premises, which underlie the following analysis, they are caught on the horns of critical dilemmas in attempting to put such requirements into practice. While the role of the pre-World War II Foreign Service was essentially political, involving negotiation and reporting, American representatives are now performing duties overseas which include the traditional functions of diplomats but also require operations in the conduct of military, economic, and informational programs. A small, homogeneous career Foreign Service was ill-equipped to meet these varied needs or to provide the leadership of personnel recruited to carry out the tasks essential to meeting the new demands. The Foreign Service, supplemented by new and more specialized "foreign services" of other agencies, entered a period of transition and instability, of growth and adaptation. It now stands in mid-passage, not yet completely aware of what its goals for development should be, certainly not adequately adapted at present even to those needs which can already be perceived.

The old Foreign Service was built on a concept of providing a number of generalists—"round pegs"—who could be rotated during a career to positions of increasing responsibility—"larger round holes"—as their experience and abilities expanded. Today's demands for personnel in agencies intimately associated with foreign affairs call not only for generalists who can direct and coordinate programs of increasingly broad scope but also for experts who can deal with detailed complexities and meet high professional standards in relatively specialized fields. Homogeneity has given way to heterogeneity among personnel serving foreign affairs agencies at home and overseas, making problems of blending the varied components—"pegs of all shapes and sizes"—extremely difficult. How to develop personnel with a greater capacity for generalization and at the same time to provide for personnel with additional specialization is a severe challenge to personnel policy-makers. There is a need to recruit and hold many specialists for lifetime careers within a speciality, yet a conflicting need to select from among these specialists some men who have the ability to transcend specialties and to assume posts requiring broad knowledge and executive ability at later points in their careers. It would appear that greater flexibility in allowing the transfer of some types of personnel for inter-agency experiences demands immediate consideration and may become a necessity on an even larger scale in the future.

The issues which are emphasized in the following analysis center around the questions of (1) whether to have a single Foreign Service or several separate services, (2) whether revised legislative authority should be sought immediately for career services in the aid and information agencies, (3) how a balance should be sought between generalist and specialist requirements, (4) what improvements might be introduced in the career recruitment process, (5) how career in-service training might be strengthened, and (6) what steps should be taken to reinforce the career management program.

ORGANIZATION: PAST AND PRESENT

Although personnel in defense and intelligence activities play important roles in foreign affairs, attention is centered here on selected problems which affect the personnel who serve in the political, aid, and information agencies. At present the Department of State, the International Cooperation Administration, and the United States Information Agency employ a total of over 23,000 American civilians, slightly more than half of whom are stationed overseas at any given time. In addition, the three agencies employ about 23,000 foreign civilians at posts or missions overseas. Approximately 13,000 of the American civilians are members of the agencies' three separate "foreign services," either as officers, reserves, or staff corps. Over 8,000 of these are serving in the Foreign Service of the United States.

A unified and professionally staffed Foreign Service was officially established by the Rogers Act of 1924. Although governed

by a Board of Foreign Service Personnel in the Department of
State, the Foreign Service was set up as an organization distinct
from the Department itself. Under the pressure for additional
specialized information, during the late 1920's and 1930's, separate
services were established by the Departments of Commerce, Agriculture, Interior, and the Treasury. The idea of a unified Foreign
Service was re-initiated in 1939 and reinforced by the Foreign
Service Act of 1946, but the Department of the Treasury continued to maintain its own service. If the Foreign Service Act was
intended as the framework for a unified Foreign Service meeting
all basic civilian needs of overseas representation, it failed to
achieve this purpose. With the aid of a friendly congressional
committee, the Department of Agriculture re-established a separate service in 1954.

The Foreign Service Act of 1946 did provide, however, for
lateral entry into the Foreign Service to make possible the recruitment of mature specialists as well as individuals with broad
general training and experience. It also created a Foreign Service
Institute which was to provide training—including some specialization—at various stages in a Foreign Service officer's career.
Neither of these steps was, or could have been, sufficient to meet
the overwhelming needs of that time. The concept of a unified
Foreign Service had to give way under the impact of cold war
programs of a military, economic, information, and intelligence
nature. Generalists in politics and diplomacy were joined overseas by increasing numbers of specialists—including many non-
career personnel—serving in separate personnel systems.

The "foreign service" of the United States Information Agency
was established by Executive Order 10477 in August 1953 after
the information service was separated from the Department of
State by Reorganization Plan 8. The "foreign service" of the Inter-
national Cooperation Administration was initiated by Policy
Directive No. 7 of May 9, 1957, signed by the Director of the
Administration. Both systems are based upon provisions of the
Foreign Service Act of 1946, but neither system has been granted

permanent or explicit legislative authority. Although the three "foreign services" face many of the same problems, they are currently at different levels of development and are organized to meet quite varied needs.

A SINGLE FOREIGN SERVICE?

With the expansion of American activities overseas after the Second World War, several proposals for the establishment of a unified career foreign affairs service were advanced. Under one such proposal, the "foreign service" systems for activities now performed by the Department of State, the International Cooperation Administration, and the United States Information Agency would have become the nucleus of such a foreign affairs service, along with the civilian personnel of the Department of Defense stationed at diplomatic missions abroad. Without prejudicing the case for or against inclusion of any civilian personnel from the Department of Defense in a career foreign affairs service, this element is excluded in consideration of the present issue: Should there be established a unified foreign affairs service, including personnel from State, ICA and USIA?

The proposal to create a unified career foreign affairs service is supported by the fact that economic and information programs are integral parts of foreign policy, and that staffs linked together in a common personnel system—in which transferability of staff is maximized—would be able to work together more effectively. The International Cooperation Administration and the United States Information Agency have already copied many aspects of the Foreign Service system in setting up their own services so, it is argued, they could easily be integrated with the Foreign Service. The provision of common personnel benefits and prerogatives might help curb discontent with present differences and create a common sense of teamwork among Americans working for these agencies in Washington and overseas. Centralized responsibility for recruitment and selection of personnel might lead to the adoption of similar personnel standards. Unification might eliminate some duplication in administrative machinery and reduce costs. It is believed that an integrated service could still accommodate different personnel needs for different kinds of programs.

Opposed to the single service proposal is the fact that the Foreign Service is still in the process of adjusting to "Wristonization" and requires additional time to become stabilized before confronting further expansion. It has also been said that uniting the three "foreign services" would be akin to merging peaches, oranges, and apples. Each agency has its different personnel needs, so administrative costs might not be greatly reduced. The present recruiting methods for the career Foreign Service, as well as its methods of selection and assignment, may be quite inapplicable to major elements of an operation like that of the International Cooperation Administration—which must continue to rely in considerable measure upon "program" staffing.[1] Of necessity, the International Cooperation Administration must "beat the bushes" in all of the professional, organization, and specialized channels from which many of its employees come. This need may require development of a decentralized system of personnel operation as in the Civil Service. The Foreign Service would be unable to undertake "program" staffing without substantial modification of its present organization and practices. Furthermore, a complete integration of personnel systems could damage the morals of International Cooperation Administration and United States Information Agency personnel who have a pride in their own organizations and do not want to be subordinated to the Foreign Service or the Department of State.

If there are excellent arguments for establishing a unified career foreign affairs service, with sufficient flexibility to meet different

[1] "Program" staffing refers to meeting personnel needs as they arise for specific programs, hiring for relatively short periods of time, often on a contract basis. Specialists so recruited sometimes serve only one two-year period overseas before returning to employment outside government. "Program" staffing makes possible the procurement of specialists possessing maturity and experience from outside government rather than requiring that such specialists be recruited at the bottom of the personnel ladder and brought to such levels within a government career system.

staffing needs, the practical problems involved in the implementation of such a step are prodigious. It should be kept in mind that the aid and information agencies are trying to build their own services along Foreign Service lines, but they are still experimenting with adaptations which appear necessary in view of the types of programs they are administering. Furthermore, the Department of State is still digesting the Wristonization experience. The United States Information Agency is working closely with the Department of State and is willing to accept unification, under conditions which meet its needs, or the present situation. Neither the International Cooperation Administration nor the Department of State, however, is interested in a further pooling of their "foreign services" in the immediate future.

Although the ultimate goal may be to establish a single service, it is useful for the time being to have the aid and information agencies work toward a common system on a relatively independent basis. The International Cooperation Administration should develop devices for cooperation with the Department of State similar to those of the United States Information Agency. The three agencies should jointly explore alternative plans by which the "foreign services" of the International Cooperation Administration and United States Information Agency could achieve closer coordination or even be unified within a modified Foreign Service so this step could be quickly implemented should it become practical and obviously advisable.

The recommendations made here do not prevent future consideration of steps beyond a "unified" service of this limited nature to a more broadly based foreign affairs service or even to an over-all government service career system of sufficient flexibility to include both domestic and foreign affairs personnel. In any adjustment of the present situation provision might well be made to allow increasing service across departmental lines both at home and abroad, according to the needs of the various agencies and the capabilities of their personnel without affecting career status adversely.

CAREER SERVICES FOR ICA AND USIA?

As a step toward the improvement of the "foreign services" of the International Cooperation Administration and the United States Information Agency, and not precluding ultimate adoption of the goal of a unified service, there is this issue: Should the International Cooperation Administration and the United States Information Agency now seek explicit legislative authority for the establishment of career services similar to the Foreign Service?

Because the International Cooperation Administration and the United States Information Agency are both considered to be "specialist" agencies, the issues involved are often treated as a single problem. Both have established makeshift services which are improvements over their earlier personnel systems, but neither has obtained specific legislative authority for the establishment of a career service comparable to the Foreign Service. The United States Information Agency has sought such legislation since mid-1954. The International Cooperation Administration, with a broader grant of operating authority, has not sought such authority.

Establishment of career services similar to the Foreign Service —but adapted to the needs of the agencies—would provide a firmer basis for attracting good recruits. The Foreign Service Reserve [2] category under which both agencies now operate implies temporary appointment which does not draw mature personnel in mid-career. Foreign Service Staff Corps assignments for officer-level positions have become virtually untenable since the Department of State removed professionals from its Foreign Service Staff Corps and uses this category primarily for administrative assistants and clerical personnel. It has been said that Foreign Service Reserve positions are too easy to terminate and the employees

[2] The Foreign Service Reserve category was created to provide for temporary appointment to the Foreign Service in cases where the Service was unable to fill job requirements from within, particularly positions requiring a degree of specialization not normally found among Foreign Service generalists. As of February 28, 1959, there were 3,456 Foreign Service officers and 841 Foreign Service Reserve officers.

have no job security, while Foreign Service Staff Corps employees in officer positions are too difficult to remove and have too much job security.

The lack of a "foreign service" in the International Cooperation Administration until 1957, which was in part responsible for the absence of any real system of rotation between headquarters and the field, left some employees overseas for many years. The result was that many of them had little knowledge of the rest of the agency and the agency exerted little control over them in the field. While it is admitted that the appointment of ICA specialists to a permanent career service would entail retraining at several points during their careers, this would be both feasible and desirable. Retraining would reduce the costs of recruiting, rehiring, and orientation. It would help keep experienced people in the field, cutting down on costly mistakes by newcomers. Those who have served abroad and adapted to overseas conditions can communicate their skills more efficiently to the people of foreign countries than can inexperienced personnel.

The United States Information Agency points with pride to its successful administration of a separate "foreign service" and believes its personnel level will rise still further with full recognition of its service. The belief is that young officers in this service have more opportunities for rapid development and assumption of responsibility than do those in the regular Foreign Service. Legislative authorization would place the Agency in a favorable recruiting position. The Agency staffs posts in many types of countries and climates and could establish a workable rotation system overseas without undue periods of service in hardship posts.

On the other hand, there is the view that a formal career service would not produce men with the zeal, the risk-taking attitude, or the innovating instinct required to implement action programs like those of these two agencies. It is said that career services build a group consciousness and feeling of superiority alien to the needs of agencies whose personnel operate largely outside of diplomatic circles. In addition, critics say, career services become protective of their members even if they are inadequate, resist changes in policy and working methods, and tend to evaluate their own performance by criteria peculiar to themselves.

More specifically, so far as the United States Information Agency is concerned, only about 200 of its 1,400-member "foreign service" are stationed in Washington at any given time. For the International Cooperation Administration the figures are about 200 out of 3,650. This fact makes any workable rotation system between headquarters and the field next to impossible. In the International Cooperation Administration, there are nearly 900 agricultural specialists in the field and only 20 or 30 positions for such technicians in Washington. The problem is made more intractable by the fact that most of the Administration's posts are "in the most unhappy and unhealthful places that ever existed." This makes continued rotation between posts overseas impractical. To bring career servants of the Administration or the United States Information Agency back to the United States for reorientation, for retraining in specialties, and for reasons of health would involve an elaborate in-service training program and/or carefully worked out placement for temporary periods in educational institutions or industries.

So far as the International Cooperation Administration is concerned, some say it really has little use for young people who would enter a career system at the Foreign Service Officer-8 level.[3] They claim that the International Cooperation Administration needs only mature personnel, in their forties and near the peak of their careers. Many believe that younger people have less skill or knowledge to communicate, are more likely to be intolerant of cultural differences, are less able to adapt American practices to techniques in underdeveloped countries, and are not accepted by foreign government officials or peoples. Supporters of this position argue for "program" rather than "career" staffing. Although the United States Information Agency can "hide" its young people doing useful tasks in embassies, they say, the International Cooper-

[3] The FSO-8 category is the class normally assigned to young men just entering a career in the Foreign Service. During their careers, the more able officers may be promoted through FSO-7, 6, 5, 4, 3, 2, and 1 to the rank of Career Minister.

Personnel Management   191

ation Administration personnel must be out in the field operating.

If the International Cooperation Administration and the United States Information Agency were given long-term status, and their programs put on a long-term basis, as recommended by the Draper Committee,[4] their personnel programs could be strengthened, even without personnel legislation. However, until they achieve such recognition, it is obvious that both organizations are working under many difficulties with their present unrecognized foreign service systems, and that they are necessarily limited in the achievement of their objectives by the shortcomings of these systems. It is equally apparent that legislatively authorized career foreign services would be costly; but this argument is in part offset by the fact that "program" staffing of International Cooperation Administration or United States Information Agency type operations is also expensive.

In view of the present and future personnel needs of these agencies and possible acceptance of the goal of a unified service, legislative authorization should be obtained for establishing separate career services for International Cooperation Administration and the United States Information Agency parallel to the Foreign Service. Consideration should also be given to providing a supplementary system of "program" staffing for elements of both agency programs. The development of the separate services should be of a nature that would not interfere with possible integration of the International Cooperation Administration and United States Information Agency services with a unified service at a later time.

BALANCE BETWEEN GENERALISTS AND SPECIALISTS

If the Foreign Service is to meet its own present needs and will possibly provide the basis for a broader future service, one issue of major importance is: How should the requirement for generalist and specialist skills be reconciled within an evolving foreign policy service?

---

[4] See *Composite Report of the President's Committee to Study the United States Military Assistance Program,* Vols. I and II (August 17, 1959), Washington, D.C.

Early in the period following the Second World War, as the Foreign Service struggled to adapt to new responsibilities, the Hoover Commission in 1949 and the Secretary of State's Advisory Committee on Personnel in 1950 recommended the establishment of an integrated Foreign Service, to be comprised of both Department of State personnel above a certain level and those already in the Foreign Service. Little implementation of these recommendations occurred until after the report of the Secretary's Public Committee on Personnel—the so-called Wriston Committee—was issued in June 1954.[5] By August 1956, "Wristonization" had been completed. The crash nature and wholesale application of the integration program was a shock to both the Department and the Foreign Service. Previous lateral entry programs had been modest in scope. Now, the concept of the Foreign Service as the special preserves of the generalists was abandoned, and the new service included specialists with training in many fields not traditionally handled by diplomats.

Although it was apparent that specialized expertise was likely to be increasingly necessary within the Foreign Service during the next decades, the first impact of Wristonization was to dilute existing expertise. Newly integrated departmental specialists in intelligence, economic policy, international organization affairs, and public affairs were sent to posts overseas where their special skills were not required and might even be lost through disuse. Foreign Service generalists were brought into the department to attempt to fill positions formerly held by specialists. Many departmental personnel were unable to adjust to fulfill representation requirements abroad, and many Foreign Service personnel needed long periods of orientation before they could even begin to meet specialized job requirements. Perhaps, as one Foreign Service officer has put it, "There is no turning back." Nevertheless, the question

---

[5] See "Toward a Stronger Foreign Service," *Report of the Secretary of State's Public Committee on Personnel,* Department of State Publication 5458, Washington, D.C. Also see Zara Steiner, *The State Department and the Foreign Service,* Princeton, N.J.: Princeton University Center of International Studies, 1958. This is the best current study of Foreign Service and Department of State personnel problems.

of how to improve integration in operation remains a real issue. A number of possible courses of action might be considered.

During the autumn of 1955, while integration was still in full swing, 205 positions which had been classified as "dual-service" posts [6]—mostly in intelligence, security, and public affairs—were returned to Civil Service status. In the first four years since the completion of Wristonization, the inclination of many has been to call for a further increase in the number of posts excepted from the Foreign Service. The pressure has been greatest in the economics and intelligence areas, but also exists in the administrative, public affairs, and international organization fields. The percentage of dual-service positions in all these categories remains relatively high.

Some critics of Wristonization have gone so far as to bemoan the loss of the old Civil Service expert from the country desks in the regional bureaus of the Department. Rational consideration of this problem is made more difficult because many of the advantages of the pre-Wristonization system were sacrificed before the advantages of the integration program could be brought to full fruition. Although the specializations which are required in various bureaus are quite different, the arguments expressed for or against an additional retreat from Wristonization are much the same throughout the Department of State.

Those calling for an increase in the number of "excepted" positions emphasize the need for continuity and expertise in many positions now classified as dual-service. It is pointed out, for example, that economists must be able to match experience with representatives of other governmental departments and of foreign governments in such technical fields as commodities, finance, and trade. It is extremely difficult to convert a Foreign Service "generalist" into an expert in these fields without years of training and experience—plus an interest in the subject matter. Foreign Service officers assigned to such posts—whether it be in economics, intelligence, or some other field—may stumble down "old blind alleys"

---

[6] Positions designated as "dual-service" were to be filled in the future by Foreign Service officers.

in search of solutions because they are ignorant of what has been done in the past, what has been carefully reviewed and found wanting. The need for continuity of relationships with personnel in other organizations is also stressed; absence of such contacts increases the time and effort that must be devoted to negotiation.

Much is made of the fact that the expertise of "Wristonees" is diluted when they are assigned to positions demanding less specialization at field posts. An excellent economic analyst specializing in raw materials trade in the Bureau of Intelligence and Research not only would lose touch with his specialty but might also make a very poor general economic reporting officer in the field. And such men are hard to replace in the Department, for they are often in demand elsewhere in government and by private employers. Yet the economic analyst, the administrative expert, the public affairs officer, or the narcotics specialist must become more of a generalist if he is to gain promotion in the Foreign Service.

Those opposed to a further increase in "excepted" positions feel that Foreign Service officers can learn most specializations required. There also is an advantage in injecting fresh insights to review old problems, particularly from the practical and comprehensive point of view of the generalists. Furthermore, as problems of foreign affairs become more complex, there will be an increasing need for an understanding of more specialized techniques by Foreign Service officers in the field. It is also hoped that mixing generalists and specialists together in the Foreign Service will improve the coordination of their efforts and increase their respect for each other.

The alternative to the proposal for a further increase in "excepted" positions is the view that the need for specialization can be met without a major retreat from Wristonization. Proponents of holding the Wristonization line advance a variety of courses of action to support their position. Careful analysis of the courses of action actually advocated by Department of State personnel is required if they are to serve as the basis for a decision on whether to continue to operate under the Wriston concept of integration of home and overseas personnel within the Foreign Service.

Advocates of lateral entry into the Foreign Service as one among several means of achieving a more satisfactory balance between generalists and specialists say that to attract mature specialists from secure positions the specialists must be given status as Foreign Service officers. They point out that because needs cannot always be foreseen, direct appointment to the Service is sometimes necessary, and that the Foreign Service has absorbed successive waves of lateral entries satisfactorily. Opponents assert that mature specialists cannot be sure until they have served whether they want to join the Foreign Service, that lateral entry delays the promotion of men who entered the Service at the bottom on a career basis, and that too much lateral entry of specialists will change the nature of the Foreign Service and make the rotation between headquarters and the field more difficult to maintain.

Supporters of a second course, temporary appointment in the Foreign Service Reserve, declare that most specialists do not want to cut their ties with outside positions until they are certain they will like the Foreign Service. Furthermore, there may be competent specialists outside the government who are interested in short or intermittent tours of duty in the Foreign Service but are certain they do not want to resign their regular positions. It is pointed out that use of the Foreign Service Reserve category allows the Foreign Service to adapt quickly to fluctuating needs, and that temporary appointments do not restrict the promotion of regular career officers. On the other hand, few reserves have been appointed to the Foreign Service until recently, and it has been difficult to keep the Reserve staffed because few specialists have been attracted by temporary appointments. As a result, Foreign Service officers are doing jobs for which they have inadequate training or little interest.

Some say that a third step, to increase the size of the Foreign Service and to establish staffing patterns which will allow the generalists time to learn specialties, has functioned well in several fields. Intelligence is cited as an example of a specialty which has not suffered unduly through the use of young Foreign Service generalists, although more men are required to do the same amount of work. This device allows the Foreign Service to expand its own "bag of tricks" by on-the-job experience. A civil servant too long on the job may become an expert in "what cannot be done" rather than in "what can be done." Civil servants often argue, however, that it takes a year to teach a Foreign Service officer the job and that before he gets to the point of making a contribution he is more interested in what his next post will be.

A fourth course of action calls for longer periods of assignment in specialist positions. This device would make the most efficient use of present specialists and allow generalists assigned to such posts to stay long enough on the job to make a contribution. It has been argued that four to eight years in a budget office would not ruin a Foreign Service officer's career as a generalist. Those opposed call attention to the officers' distaste for many special tasks. Specialization may also require more sophisticated training than can be given on the job. This course of action would also retard the rotation system.

A fifth approach would give specialists in the Foreign Service career opportunities equal to those of generalists. Use of Wristonees from the administrative field as Deputy Chiefs of Mission is cited as one example of the many possibilities to equalize opportunities. In addition, if there are specialists who have highly valued and rare technical skills, there should be ways of providing them with adequate remuneration without moving them into positions involving top-level executive responsibilities. By such means, the Service might permit specialization for some throughout a career which would provide the degree of expertise which the competitive world situation now demands. Others, however, believe that specialists cannot blend their efforts with the Foreign Service teams unless they have had a variety of experiences. They point to the limited number of posts at the top now available to specialists, and they add that most leaders are men who started out as specialists and became generalists.

A sixth suggestion emphasizes the need for in-service training as a means of developing specialization within the Service. It takes into consideration the need for re-tooling of specialists at various points in their careers if they are to keep abreast of the latest developments in their fields. This approach could be implemented without hampering promotional opportunities for career officers. On the other hand, training for specialization after entry into the Foreign Service is a costly process, involving expenditures for instruction and the loss of a man in an operating job. Furthermore, training takes time, while the need for specialists may be immediate.

A seventh proposal calls for a thorough inventory of what present capabilities are available within the Service and what future needs will be; on that basis steps would be taken to fill the gap by training or recruiting. It is suggested that the study should be continuing because needs will fluctuate and cannot be foreseen with sufficient accuracy to rely upon a single analysis. Those opposed point to the impossibility of foreseeing the future, thus claiming that both world conditions and the tasks to be performed by the Foreign Service may change. They argue that it is better to be practical and meet needs as they arise, without wasteful expenditure for training specialists who may never be needed.

An eighth course of action proposes that, because specialized talents are not given recognition by the Foreign Service examination, the examination should be revised so that appropriate specialists will be drawn into the Service. It is said that some change in the examination is needed to make it reflect the needs of the future instead of those of the past. Opponents feel that such a restructuring of the examination might not bring in young officers who would be best adapted for performing as generalists—for whom there will be a continuing demand. Changing the nature of the examination might reduce the numbers taking it because students traditionally interested in the Foreign Service have had a relatively broad liberal arts background—rather than a high degree of specialization—largely in the fields of political science, history, economics and international relations.

A review of these courses of action in support of Wristonization and of the arguments for a further increase in "excepted" positions within the Department indicates that no one course of action provides the whole answer to the call for more "exceptions." Some of them will help to meet immediate needs; others, long-range needs. Obviously, it will be necessary to combine elements of several of the suggested courses of action to achieve a forward-looking program which will maintain a degree of flexibility sufficient to meet any eventuality. To this end, certain general recommendations can be suggested.

There should be only limited or temporary additional exceptions from the Wristonization program. One of at least five criteria should be met before any additional positions are excepted from the Foreign Service:

1. Is the position a narrow specialty of little use in enriching the experience of a Foreign Service officer? Certain disbursing positions, for example, might fall within such a category.

2. Is the position so indirectly related to foreign policy formulation or implementation that its occupant will derive little benefit from the broadening experience of assignment to the field? Again, disbursing is a prime example. Budgeting would not be included in this category.

3. Is the position a narrow specialty which requires such knowledge that after service abroad reassignment to a position in the Department would require more than three months of re-training?

4. Is the position such a narrow specialty or does it require such broad competence that no officer now in the Foreign Service and available for assignment could fill it with six months or less of training or on-the-job orientation?

5. Is there no officer-level staff-member in an organizational unit—say a division or even a branch—who can provide adequate continuity with the past or sufficient continuity of relationships with outside organizations with which the unit must deal? This might apply to certain intelligence and administrative units as well as to some involving relationships with the public or multilateral organizations. It should be emphasized that in each instance the burden of proof should rest upon those requesting the exception. No widespread de-integration should be necessary.

In view of the rejection of any major shift in the balance between dual-service and excepted positions, the following steps might be taken:

1. Lateral entry into the Foreign Service or appointments in the Foreign Service Reserve should be made as necessary without reluctance but not regarded as the major means of acquiring specialists. However, requirements for such lateral entry should be flexible and realistic and not prevent the procurement of the best specialists available or exceptionally able generalists because of ill-conceived limitations. For example, the ability of a specialist or generalist procured at mid-career to pass a language examination or to pass the entry examination given to prospective FSO-8's may not be relevant to the job which only he may be able to do.

2. The possibility of giving longer tours of duty to personnel assigned to specialist positions should be carefully explored.

3. Opportunities for service at the rank of Career Minister should be opened in many special fields, with no prejudice against promotion of specialists to this rank.

4. Specialists should be developed within the Foreign Service in instances where the proper talent is discovered, and in-service training should be provided to re-tool and maintain expertise during a specialist's career.

5. There should be a continuing review of capabilities and needs, and of methods for adapting to future demands.

6. Foreign Service examinations should be drawn up and administered so that potential generalists will not be penalized, but with an opportunity for a limited number of specialists to be selected each year through similar but somewhat differently structured examinations.

If the Foreign Service is to staff a wide range of operational and specialized program posts in the future, it cannot hope to select talented young blood to fill these positions by a single examination.

RECRUITMENT

Another continuing issue is: How can the recruitment program at the beginning level (Class 8) be improved? The Wriston Committee's report of May 1954 recommended four steps for improving the recruitment of young officers at the bottom of the career ladder. It called for increased recruitment over a broader geographical area, with state quotas set in accordance with population; a shorter entrance examination offered at centers throughout the country; a strengthened liaison program with colleges and universities; and a Foreign Service scholarship training program similar to the Navy's contract system for its Reserve Officer Corps.

Although the Department of State has not pressed for the establishment of a quota system to increase the representative nature of the Foreign Service, the geographic distribution of entering Foreign Service officers has broadened. In part, this has been the result of an increased liaison program with colleges and universities and the new type of entrance examination offered at centers throughout the country.

There is little need to worry further about increasing geographic distribution. This will probably occur naturally as the involvement of the United States in foreign affairs continues and as more Americans become interested in foreign policy. Fluctuations in the annual intake of junior officers, however, remains a problem in the maintenance of liaison with the academic world. Plans should be made so that the annual examination will not be eliminated again, nor made too difficult for candidates to pass.

The new examination process has itself raised problems. The objective written examination is structured in different ways to favor those with certain subject matter backgrounds. This may help meet the changing needs of the Foreign Service, but it makes it difficult for college students to plan an educational program in preparation for a Foreign Service career. (Many young men interested in the traditional diplomatic and reporting activities of the Foreign Service now hesitate to enter upon a Foreign Service career because of the large percentage of young careerists who are assigned to minor administrative posts, such as disbursing. The increase in administrative assignments stems from the Department of State's responsibility to provide administrative services backstopping other government agencies operating overseas. It is because of this situation that the United States Information Agency believes it offers young people greater opportunities than the Foreign Service.) Whenever there is a need for Foreign Service recruits with area, language, or functional specialization, provision should be made for separate and specially structured examinations to select them. Recruits thus selected would normally follow special career patterns, except in those instances where they might develop and display outstanding capacity for broader types of service.

The one-day multiple choice test instituted in 1955 de-emphasized the need for formal training in international relations and eliminated any direct test of the candidate's ability to write. The need to give Foreign Service officers selected by such an examination some formal training in international relations should be recognized by an expansion of the in-service training program. Because officers are often assigned to reporting or drafting duties, reliance upon an objective test may not provide sufficient indication of a candidate's ability in written expression.

Oral examinations are now offered in many different cities by examination panels of varied composition and abilities. Ratings are scarcely standardized; yet the order of appointment is determined entirely by the numerical score on the oral examination, with no account taken of the results of the written examination. Even if the quality of examination panels is controlled and improved, this practice would appear to be both unfair and unrealistic. It is particularly unfortunate under present conditions in view of the backlog of candidates who have in recent years had to wait long periods for appointments. The lack of assurance that those taking the Foreign Service examination will be promptly informed whether they have passed or failed, and at what time they can be given a definite appointment, remains an obstacle. If there are a dedicated few who will endure unlimited trials in order to get into the Service, there are others who are equally interested but unwilling to join an organization which so patently displays its inability to meet a basic and reasonable personnel need.

The Wriston Committee's suggestion of a scholarship training program as a means of stimulating preparation for the Foreign

Service has not been implemented. In part, this is because under the new examination procedure only a general liberal arts background is required. The Department has been able to find plenty of such graduates to take the examination. Whether their interest is as deep and abiding in foreign affairs as candidates brought in by the pre-1955 examinations remains to be seen. There is some feeling in the Department of State and the Foreign Service that the new system has resulted in a lowering of entry standards. Perhaps such a downgrading of standards was temporarily necessary in view of the expanding needs of the Service and the previous shortage of qualified applicants to take the examination. However, it may once again be advisable for the examination and recruitment process to give preference to the person who has some personal commitment to the idea of work in government and in foreign affairs, and who has demonstrated this devotion over a period of time by securing an education relevant to the fulfillment of that purpose, particularly at the graduate level.

This raises a related question. Should the government create its own undergraduate Foreign Service Academy, the graduates of which would be eligible for appointment to the Foreign Service without examination? Several such measures are now before the Congress. The major assumption underlying such a proposal is that there is a need for special training which is not presently available and which could best be furnished in a governmental academy. It is argued that individuals trained in such an institution would be "committed" to a Foreign Service career, thus assisting the Department of State to compete more successfully with other employers for top caliber young men. It is pointed out that liberal arts institutions are not likely to equal such an academy in the attention or resources they would be willing to devote to foreign policy training.

If the standards of the Foreign Service examination were returned to their pre-1955 level—when some formal training in international relations was normally necessary in order to pass—the Department of State might have some difficulty in securing a large number of applicants to take the examination. It has been said that when the Department could not find a sufficient number of candidates with both knowledge and personality, it sacrificed knowledge for personality in the hope of providing in-service training to remedy this deficiency. Staffing patterns have prevented the participation of entering officers in an in-service training program adequate to meet this new need, and in-service training has not expanded rapidly enough to provide the educational background which should be a prerequisite for membership in the Foreign Service.

Opponents of the Foreign Service Academy declare that the cost would be high, that persons trained in this manner would become a distinct clique, and that there is no shortage of applicants for entry into the Foreign Service. Some who oppose an Academy are satisfied with the caliber of officers entering the Foreign Service. Others point to the possibility that appointment would be by political selection more than merit and that admission based on quotas by population might—with less interest in such an Academy in some parts of the country than others—result in graduates of quite different levels of ability. More significantly, it is argued that the Foreign Service requires persons with diverse educational backgrounds. Such diversity can only be provided by drawing on the widely varied resources of liberal arts institutions. The Foreign Service has been criticized enough for being "a closed club" and a "protective association" without encouraging "separatism" by establishing a special Foreign Service Academy. A telling argument in opposition to establishment of a Foreign Service Academy is the obvious fact that it is hard enough to select personnel in their twenties who have the potential for development to the rank of Career Minister. The process of selection might be even more difficult if it had to be made while applicants were still in their teens. The most practical reason for rejecting the idea of an undergraduate academy is the fact that the Foreign Service often finds candidates at the minimum age level for acceptance possessing real ability but lacking sufficient maturity to fulfill its functions and must recommend further education or employment experience before actual induction.

Automatic acceptance of academy graduates would tend to force a most unfortunate "wet nursing" function upon the Foreign Service, the Department of State, and other agencies using such an Academy as a source of recruitment.

It seems clear that many of the points advanced in support of an undergraduate Foreign Service Academy can be met by steps which do not have the disadvantages of such a governmental Foreign Service Academy. For example, it appears that a broad merit scholarship training program—particularly at the graduate level—would provide a significant number of applicants for entry into the Foreign Service with equal or better formal training and at less cost than an undergraduate academy without creating a Foreign Service "type." A functioning scholarship program of this nature would enable the Foreign Service to reinstitute some of the requirements of the pre-1955 examination, and would raise the standards of knowledge without any undue sacrifice in maturity or in personality characteristics. Under these circumstances, it would be neither necessary nor advisable to create a governmental undergraduate Foreign Service Academy. While a substantial job of in-service training would still remain to be done after induction of young FSO-8's into the Foreign Service, such a program is both feasible and desirable.

IN-SERVICE TRAINING

With regard to in-service training, the main questions are: How much time should be devoted to such formal training during an officer's career, at what stages should it be offered, to what categories of personnel, and in what kinds of institutions—governmental or non-governmental?

Officers entering the Foreign Service on a career basis have traditionally been drawn from among the graduates of Eastern liberal arts colleges, although recent recruitment figures indicate a much broader geographic base. Even with a college level of education at entry, further in-service training has proved to be a necessity. The Foreign Service Act of 1946 provided for the creation of a

Foreign Service Institute, but the Institute's program was at low ebb in 1954 when the Wriston Committee issued its recommendations, including several for strengthening in-service training. It was possible at that time for senior officers in the Foreign Service to have completed their formal education twenty years earlier, to have been busily engaged during the interim period in rotation between a series of practical assignments, and because of their preoccupations to be almost totally unaware of the relationship of new concepts and methods in the social and behavioral sciences to an understanding of international relations. It was also possible for them to be unaware of the potential impact of scientific and technological advances upon the formulation and conduct of American foreign policy.[7] Located in the Office of the Deputy Under Secretary of State for Administration since March 8, 1955, the Foreign Service Institute has taken rapid strides toward eliminating such vacuums of knowledge, but much remains to be done.

Emphasis is now placed upon an introductory orientation course, language training, a mid-career course, and a senior officer course. In addition, a limited number of Foreign Service officers are assigned for training outside the Institute, attending university graduate schools or governmental institutions like the service-sponsored senior war colleges, the National War College, and the British Imperial Defense College. The training skeleton is there, but meat needs to be put on the bones if future requirements of the Foreign Service are to be met.

The Institute's in-service training program still falls short of those offered by any of the armed services.[8] This will not be reme-

[7] For a discussion of the relationship of and impact of this knowledge, see "Possible Nonmilitary Scientific Developments and Their Potential Impact on Foreign Policy Problems of the United States." (A study prepared at the request of the Committee on Foreign Relations, United States Senate, by the Stanford Research Institute, September, 1959.) Washington: Government Printing Office, 1959.

[8] See "Recruitment and Training for the Foreign Service of the United States." (A staff study for the Committee on Foreign Relations, United States Senate.) Washington, D.C.: Government Printing Office, 1958.

died until Foreign Service officers at all levels recognize the new needs of the Service and cease to be reluctant to intersperse tours of duty with educational assignments. Present staffing patterns —based on a false sense of economy—make it difficult to free officers for training. Appropriations for training remain low compared to the job that should be done. Much of the teaching is done as a gesture of goodwill by governmental employees taking time off from their regular duties, by single appearances of experts from outside government, by non-professional educators drawn from the Foreign Service, or by ill-paid tutors with little job security. This is not to say that some excellent teaching is not done in the Institute; it is only to suggest that the program can and should be better.

One in-service training question is: How much time should be devoted during a career to formal training assignments? Most courses at the Foreign Service Institute are of the "shock treatment" type, covering broad areas in two or three weeks. Few Foreign Service officers are assigned to training programs of as long as nine months at a single time; currently there are only about 90 to 100 per year so assigned, out of almost 3,500. Few officers have spent as much as two years in formal full-time training assignments during prolonged periods of service. The Army estimates that the average military officer with a career of 28 years will spend 3.2 years in training. The comparison is not flattering to the Foreign Service. Temporarily, as a result of implementation of the language training program on a crash basis, about 9 per cent of the total Foreign Service man-years are going into training. This is expected to fall to 6 per cent when the language program tapers off. In other words, the current program is running at the rate of 2.7 years of training per officer in a 30-year career, and it is scheduled subsequently to drop back to 1.8 years of training per officer. In an increasingly complex world, it would seem desirable to move toward the academic concept of the sabbatical year, one year in seven, for training as a minimal objective to set for the average officer in the Foreign Service. Officers slated for high policy-making positions might be allowed an additional year at two separate stages in their careers for independent study and reflection in an academic atmosphere outside formal training programs.

At what stages in the careers of Foreign Service officers should in-service training be provided? Training is now given at several stages during a Foreign Service officer's career. If there were an increase in time allocated for in-service training during the next ten or fifteen years, additional levels or expanded training at given levels might be anticipated. Among the alternative levels at which full-time in-service training might be given are the following, roughly in stepping-stone order through a career:

1. basic orientation course following induction;

2. rotational on-the-job experiences within the Department as a first working assignment;

3. assignment to a governmental or non-governmental institution to complete a graduate degree or degrees after a probationary period of about five years;

4. specialized area and language training before assignment to a foreign country for the first time, if needed;

5. training in the performance of a specific functional task before assignment to duty (This might occur at several stages.);

6. rotational on-the-job experiences within an embassy on first assignment overseas;

7. rotational on-the-job experiences between the Department and one or more other agencies early in career (This might also occur at later stages.);

8. "mid-career" training involving Foreign Service officers and representatives of other agencies;

9. training in the Foreign Service Institute senior officer course or its equivalent;

10. training at the National War College or some other advanced inter-departmental training school.

Without a review of each alternative, it may be pointed out that some of these levels of training are in existence at the present time. For example, candidates who have passed the Foreign Service examination—written and oral—are often encouraged to pursue graduate study at their own, rather than at governmental, expense. Even more serious, there is little opportunity for rotational on-the-job experiences in other agencies. Although no one officer under present staffing patterns can be spared for participation in all such training programs, short as most of them now are, the well-rounded Foreign Service officer who is to serve in positions of top leadership would benefit from each experience.

Who should participate in a balanced Foreign Service in-service training program? There is no problem in determining that all incoming officers should take part in some kind of orientation course. The current question is who should be assigned to the mid-career and senior officer courses. At present, the goal is to run the top 35 per cent of the officers through the 12-week mid-career course. Actually, only 22 per cent of all officers in Classes 4, 5, and 6 are receiving such training. Other officers receive language and area training or specialized advanced training in economics or political science instead of the mid-career course, but no more than 35 per cent of all officers receive one of these various courses at mid-career. By 1962, it is planned that 6 per cent of the officers in Classes 2 and 3 will have taken the senior officer course. Between two and three times as many will have attended one of the senior war colleges. This would indicate that no more than 25 per cent of the officers in these classes will have had a senior level training course by 1962.

There are several possible alternatives for determining who should receive mid-career and senior training:

1. Only outstanding officers at each level might be selected for training.

2. All officers might be trained at mid-career and a high percentage might receive senior training.

3. Officers might be selected for training on the basis of need for improvement, with average or below-average officers being given preference.

The Department has finally been able to implement the first alternative after a number of years during which assignment for training was used both as a means of rewarding the best officers and as a repository for weaker ones. With an effective "promotion-up, selection-out" system,[9] there would be little advantage to be gained by adopting the third alternative. In practice, few have been "selected-out" of, or removed from, the Foreign Service. Thus a good case can be made for giving training to all officers at mid-career because few are likely to be selected-out before a number of years of additional service. Senior officers are serving and will serve in such important posts that the benefits they may derive from training will have considerable impact upon the conduct of foreign policy. Those with more than five years ahead before retirement should probably be assigned senior level training. To meet future needs, therefore, the second alternative appears most attractive.

In addition to general participation in the orientation, mid-career, and senior officer courses, Foreign Service officers should be assigned to language, area, functional, and most other training courses on the basis of the training prerequisites for positions to which they are assigned. This would require explicit designation of the training prerequisites for all positions to be filled by Foreign Service officers. If such a study is made on a realistic basis, it will undoubtedly indicate the need for a reinforced program of in-service training. Assignment for independent study and reflection might well be reserved for the officers marked for promotion to the highest policy-making positions.

Aside from the matter of the possible Foreign Service Academy, there is the general question: In what kinds of institutions—governmental or non-governmental—should in-service training be given?

The advantages of in-service training in governmental institutions include free access to classified source material and association with other students of similar interest and training, including representatives of other governmental agencies. The curriculum and procedures have tended to have a practical orientation, and

[9] The Foreign Service personnel system requires either promotion to a higher class within a specified number of years or removal from the Service. Thus, it is commonly called a "promotion-up, selection-out" system.

training can be scheduled in brief periods adapted to stringent staffing patterns.

While the universities may lack classified source materials, they normally have better research facilities and traditions than governmental institutions. The Foreign Service officer assigned to an academic institution comes into contact with graduate students possessing a wide diversity of views. His contact with professors is more sustained. The approach is likely to bring basic concepts of the social and behavioral sciences to bear on immediate practical issues. Training is usually for periods of at least one and possibly two or more semesters, escaping the capsule nature of many governmental courses.

In the past, graduate-level training was not considered essential for Foreign Srvice officers, although those who entered the Service by regular examination procedures generally have attained a higher educational level than Wristonees or other lateral entrants. (See table, "Levels of Educational Attainment in the Foreign Service," June, 1959). It is still true that the degrees themselves are of little use for governmental careers, but as the need for specialized training mounts and as the complexities of foreign affairs problems grow, additional graduate-level training will become a necessity—whether in a non-governmental or governmental institution, whether in quest of an advanced degree or not. It is difficult to say what the proper balance between training in governmental and non-governmental institutions should be. In most cases, probably a mixture is best, adjusted to the needs of the Service and the individual.

IMPROVEMENT OF CAREER MANAGEMENT

A related issue is: Is there a need for revising the program of career management in the Foreign Service for the evaluation or rating of performance, for assignment, and for promotion-up or selection-out?

A formal career management program in the Foreign Service was started from scratch after the Wriston Committee made its

Levels of Educational Attainment in the Foreign Service
(June, 1959)

	Examination Group No.	%	Wriston Group No.	%	Other Lateral Entrants No.	%	Total No.	%
High school graduate, but less than bachelor's degree or equivalent	45	2.85	430	30.43	36	11.61	511	15.45
Bachelor's degree, but less than master's degree or equivalent	969	61.17	600	42.46	144	46.45	1,713	51.80
Master's degree, but less than Ph.D. degree or equivalent	517	32.64	279	19.75	84	27.10	880	26.61
Ph.D. degree or more	53	3.34	104	7.36	46	14.84	203	6.14
Total	*1,584*	*100.00*	*1,413*	*100.00*	*310*	*100.00*	*3,307*	*100.00*

(This table is based on Department of State statistics. The educational levels of one from the Examination Group and nine from the Wriston Group were not indicated and are omitted from the above computations.)

recommendations. The most promising aspect of this program was the establishment of a Career Development and Counseling Staff as part of the Office of Personnel within the Department of State. The Staff is off to an excellent start, but it does not bear the responsibility for all aspects of career management.

Singled out as problem areas requiring consideration and further action are the following: (1) the evaluation and rating of the performance of Foreign Service personnel, (2) the methods by which personnel are assigned to duty, and (3) the promotion-up, selection-out system.

It is alleged that officers newly integrated into the Foreign Service—the "Wristonees"—have suffered when rated by "regular" Foreign Service supervisors. Many long-time Foreign Service officers feel that they have also been held back at some point in their careers by unfair ratings. The Department is only beginning to study the "rating history" of supervising officers on a tentative basis; such a study should be a first step toward improving the evaluation system and putting such charges to rest.

A further development of the Foreign Service Inspection Corps, which makes independent ratings of Foreign Service officers as a check on supervisory officers who rate personnel, might also be helpful. The Inspection Corps appears to be understaffed for the importance of the functions it performs.

It is alleged that pressure can be brought to bear after assignments not to an officer's liking have been made—if he has the proper friends—so that he can be reassigned to a post he prefers. It is charged that some Foreign Service officers spend an undue amount of time during tours of duty in Washington cultivating those whom they believe can obtain "favorable" assignments for them. The only possible conclusion is that steps should be taken to ensure that assignments are made on an objective basis. If assignment panels can be developed which are composed of Foreign Service officers who possess a reputation for objectivity and some specialization in career management, these panels should consult with regional or functional bureaus of the Department before definite determination of assignment is made, but their decisions after such consultation should be final and not subject to non-rational pressures or review. It should be recognized that the proper performance of the assignment function will become less difficult if staffing patterns become less stringent and the quality of personnel less uneven within Foreign Service classes or ranks.

The selection-out process has not been strictly administered. Officers have been kept in the Foreign Service who were scheduled for selection-out because early retirement benefits were not considered adequate. If there is too much "deadweed" in the Foreign Service or too many officers in the higher ranks, the principles of promotion-up, selection-out should, perhaps, be applied with greater vigor. After an interim period, however, the question of whether or not to place continued reliance upon the present promotion-up, selection-out system should be carefully reconsidered. Selection-out at any point during a career may be less necessary if methods of selection for entry into the Service are further refined and if the possibility of selection-out is retained during a probationary period of about five years.

With the increasing training needs of the Foreign Service and with additional funds required for the education of each individual officer, application of the promotion-up, selection-out process later in the career may become too wasteful to continue. Older officers may perform many lower-level jobs more ably and be more satisfied doing them than younger men on their way up the promotion ladder. If promotion were not a requirement for remaining in the Foreign Service, officers might display a bit more independence of thought and be less afraid to present original ideas. In a mature personnel system, the "flue" remains open for rapid promotion of outstanding young men without application of the selection-out principle. Separation for good reason would still be possible and could be administered in such a way as to eliminate personnel unfit for further service. The conclusion here would be to place more emphasis on good recruitment and career development and to worry less about implementing present selection-out regulations.

Conclusions

Many of the arguments advanced in opposition to positive steps proposed to improve personnel in the foreign affairs agencies seem to stem from a failure to realize the traumatic changes which the Foreign Service has already passed through, and its potential if sufficient provision is made for further adaptation to meet the needs of the future. The Foreign Service and the new career "foreign services" of other agencies are sometimes opposed for what the Foreign Service may have been when it was meeting the needs of another time, rather than for what it now is or can become.

Certainly the old Foreign Service did not provide an adequate number of top-level executive personnel who could assume responsibility for coordinating policy-decisions in Washington or their implementation overseas. Products of an adaptive Foreign Service and the new career "foreign services," trained and developed in this modern and rather complex period, are more likely to provide a reservoir of both generalist and specialist personnel adequate to the tasks of leadership which lie ahead—if personnel policy-makers in both the executive and legislative branches of the government are foresighted.

For leavening purposes, there will always need to be a sprinkling of "outsiders" with broad interests and exceptional ability who are not permanently associated with any foreign affairs career system serving in foreign affairs positions. However, the major personnel needs of the foreign affairs agencies in the future—except for technicians and some extremely narrow specialists who will continue to be recruited by "program" staffing—must be largely met by evolving a flexible and dynamic career personnel system.

10 Finale
Washington, Delegation, Coordination

The Clank and the Creaks

The need for new ideas to help resolve problems of broad and narrow scope, of long- and short-term nature, is now recognized at several levels within the Department of State and here and there throughout the government. This is a hopeful sign, but the creation of an idea mechanism within the policy machine would be a step toward solution of only one among many problems which American policy-makers confront in adapting our national behavior to a world in crisis. The noisy clank in the operation of the policy machine, caused by the lack of an adequate mechanism to provide a continuing challenge to its basic assumptions or broader goals, almost drowns out a number of serious administrative creaks which also demand attention and repair, like those dealt with in the chapter on personnel management. The very dimensions and complexity of the policy-making machinery, only a small portion of which has been singled out for description and analysis here, make it difficult to comprehend or come to grips with the full gamut of problems important to national survival.

The "D.C." in Washington, D.C., could stand for "delegation" and "coordination." If these are the twin cardinal principles of good public administration, it is easier to accept this fact than to put it into practice. As a result, the Department of State and the other foreign affairs agencies are constantly wrestling with problems of delegation and coordination, both internally and in their relations with each other. Four problem areas related to one or the other of the two principles are singled out to conclude this analysis of Department of State policy-making in its government-wide setting: (1) delegation of decision-making within the Department of State, (2) matching policies and funds in the budget process, (3) coordination of the foreign affairs agencies by the President, and (4) the Department of State's future—coordinated or coordinator?

DELEGATION IN THE DEPARTMENT

The problem of delegation is not peculiar to the Department of State; the assumption of needlessly heavy work-loads by top officials is a government-wide phenomenon. Most government problems cannot be solved, only resolved. Some believe the over-involvement in detail is a psychological response to this fact by men who are attempting to prove they are doing all they can to meet their responsibilities to the nation. It should also be realized that men who reach these high positions have a tremendous drive for and interest in "power." They may tend to create "empires" of responsibility at the expense of competitors who also seek power. Others attribute the problem to a lack of administrative experience or knowledge.

An increasing flow of paper is being generated by the policy machine for consideration by the Department's senior officers. In 1954, only about 500 staff studies per month reached the offices of the Secretary and Under Secretary of State.[1] By 1958, the figure had increased to approximately 850 per month. There is a flood of paper at the desk level in the regional bureaus, as already noted, and at every other level up to and including the Secretary. The Secretary and Under Secretary deal with over forty staff studies per day as compared to only twenty-five per day five years ago. A continuation of this trend will require the delegation of some duties—decision-making or otherwise—to Department officials of lower rank. If the Under Secretary for Political Affairs and the Deputy Under Secretary for Administration take on any addi-

---

[1] A staff study is a paper relating to a single problem, sent up to one of the two senior officers through the Executive Secretariat of the Department, for information or action.

tional burdens, they in turn must delegate decisions they have been making to the Assistant Secretaries and so on down the line. Such a step would require a careful delineation of authority for action on all major types of questions, plus an ability on the part of each Assistant Secretary to whom the power of decision is delegated to take into account the views of others at his own level without taking the cutting-edge off his decisions.

Top Department officers are now dealing with details of limited significance which are pushed to abnormal heights. If a unit in the Department is dissatisfied with a decision, it presses the question to a higher level and forces reconsideration. Senior officers must then be briefed before they can act. This is often a waste of time. Furthermore, it undercuts the authority of the lower officers who should be making a high percentage of such decisions. With proper devices for coordination and with personnel of adequate intellectual stature, training, and experience, plus will and determination, this adjustment of decision-making to lower levels may be satisfactorily achieved. The shift will not be an easy one and there will be some sour decisions with accompanying headaches in the process. Even under the most favorable circumstances, delegation is not likely to proceed any faster than absolutely necessary; so, there is little likelihood that the Secretary, Under Secretary, Under Secretary for Political Affairs, or the Deputy Under Secretary for Administration will acquire any substantial amount of thinking time which would enable them to look beyond the next emergency which threatens the national interest.

The Assistant Secretary of a regional or functional bureau is already a heavily burdened individual, in most instances, except where he is a good administrator and has made proper delegation to subordinates while a senior officer is reaching down and taking over many of his responsibilities. Before the average Assistant Secretary can assume additional responsibilities, the levels of decision-making in the bureaus will have to be thoroughly overhauled and the quality of their personnel up-graded to enable them to assume a major portion of the crushing workload already threatening the efficiency of most of those serving at the Assistant

Secretary level. The problem may partially be one of obtaining suitable personnel. Do we have a sufficient number of persons who can assume decision-making tasks, amply trained in breadth and depth, who are willing to make the sacrifices of time, energy, and monetary reward which will be demanded of them in the service of their country? Office Directors and desk officers may be adequate in many cases to handle the current level of decisions and the present workload. Can they absorb additional policy-making responsibilities or fruitfully increase the length of their working days, their usual ten-hour day five days a week, plus Saturday and Sunday mornings? It can only be said that the desk officer now tends to work less than the Office Director, and the Office Director less than the Assistant Secretary, and that there are more relatively "quiet periods" in a particular country or group of countries than within an entire continent.

The tendency of an Assistant Secretary to enter into too many decisions within his bureau, to reach too far down and spread himself too thin, may be stimulated by the rather elaborate staffs which now cluster around each Assistant Secretary in addition to the bureau's Office Directors. It would seem essential for the Assistant Secretary to delegate to the regional-wide offices additional decisions of a political or economic nature where a large number of countries are involved or where the action taken will have implications across sub-regional office lines. Delegation should be made to the sub-regional offices where the problems primarily affect the states within a sub-region. Such delegation might enable the Assistant Secretary to take on additional responsibilities from above. Hopefully, it might free him to face broader regional problems in a more forward-looking manner. To recommend delegation of authority to lower levels at a time when greater coordination of policy is necessary both among the bureaus of the Department and by the Department with other agencies of the government may appear at first to be inconsistent. It may not really be. If policy-making officers at higher levels could be freed for the consideration of only the most important problems and for the projection of a sense of direction to those serving under them, their guidance to those who would bear greater responsibility at lower levels might counter any loss of coordination resulting from a carefully spelled-out delegation of decision-making authority.

BUDGETING: MATCHING POLICIES AND FUNDS

The most anachronistic, least understood part of the whole government mechanism influencing the substance of American foreign policy is the budget process. Foreign policies, whether they be of a political, military, economic, or informational nature, require personnel and material for their implementation. People and goods cost money. It is relatively simple to draw up grand plans and policies in individual agencies, bureaus, or missions overseas; it is more difficult to establish priorities among such plans, to allocate scarce resources in a fashion which will best further the interests of the United States—foreign and domestic —on both a short- and long-range basis. Although the Bureau of the Budget exists in the executive branch to assist the President in matching policies and funds, it is doubtful if it is adequately staffed or organized to meet the needs of the present, let alone those of the more difficult future. Within each department or agency, "budget shops" attempt to achieve a similar balance between policies and funds.

Unfortunately, the lines of communication between policy-makers and the budget people in government are often—if not usually—imperfect. Policy-makers at all levels tend to ignore budget considerations, and often reach decisions without understanding the total costs involved, without determining whether a new policy has sufficient value to give it priority over another which must be curtailed if it is adopted. National Security Council policies approved by President Harry Truman but left as an un-implemented residue to the Eisenhower administration are said to have been "costed out" at $20,000,000,000—to everyone's surprise. Tops among such "horror stories" is the one told of a recent peace-time year when the Joint Chiefs of Staff asked military policy-makers to make budget requests for everything they really needed. The unscreened requests totaled $120,000,000,000. It is little wonder that the Bureau of the Budget and the "budget shops" in most of the foreign affairs agencies—including the Department of State —are considered "stingy" by the policy-makers, that policy-makers are considered "financially irresponsible" by the budgeteers in the Bureau of the Budget and the agency budget shops. Further complicating the budget process is the fact that funds must in many cases—for example, the Mutual Security Program—first be authorized and then appropriated by separate committees in both the Senate and the House of Representatives, and that the funds to cover these appropriations must be raised by yet a third committee in each chamber of the legislative branch.

Harassed by the necessity of seeking annual authorizations and appropriations for major programs, and forced to obligate most of the funds appropriated in a single year, in spite of complex limitations placed on the use of funds, many executive branch employees believe that the Congress has impaired the effectiveness of the foreign affairs programs. On the other hand, there are those in the legislative branch who feel that the executive branch has too much freedom, that the Congress ought to control and instruct even more in the future than in the past.

No one denies that the budget process is complicated and needs to be simplified and made more realistic. The time from the first request by an agency budget shop for "flash estimates" on a new budget to the receipt of an allotment for the first quarter of a fiscal year by a bureau in a foreign affairs agency in Washington or a mission in the field may be some sixteen to eighteen months. In the meantime, the budget has been filtered through some forty-five levels of authority—not counting internal processes within a level, such as take place within the Office of Budget in the Department of State. Amid swiftly moving international events, a foreign affairs agency may find itself operating near the close of a fiscal year on a budget for which plans were initiated some twenty-five months earlier. There is small wonder that funds are not always immediately available to meet the current needs of foreign affairs agencies.

There is said to be an acute lack of faith between each level in the budgetary process within the executive branch, with the level above trying to find hidden "pokes" and the level below trying to hoard in such a way that it can operate even if cuts are imposed. It is claimed that a spiraling fixation on detail and increasing mutual distrust have been set off by the continuing interplay of "devious devices" concocted at one end of Pennsylvania Avenue and the "picayune probes" conducted at the other. As a result, there are those who believe that both the executive and legislative branches need to be reminded that they should not lose track of policy purposes in an endless display of gamesmanship and inter-hierarchal nit-picking.

The annual "battle of the budget" interlards dramatic skirmishes over basic policy issues of national importance with haggling on points of minor administrative significance. It demands the time of the President, Department Secretaries, and congressional leaders, as well as that of hundreds of anonymous "little people" toiling in agency budget shops or on the staffs of congressional committees. It produces more reading matter than even a scholar is likely to read in a year—the President's budget of 2,000 pages and Congressional hearings of some 25,000 pages. The budget process is complex and time-consuming, gives conscious satisfaction to few of those who participate in it, and has led many to ask the question: is this the best way to get the job done? The answer to this question may be that the trip is sometimes necessary but that it doesn't have to be made by covering all the back routes by wagon train in this era of Cadillacs, thruways, and intercontinental ballistic missiles.

Three types of improvement in the budgetary field would remedy many of the present shortcomings. Those suggested most often are (1) better personnel, (2) a shorter, simpler budget process, and (3) authorization and availability of funds for periods of more than one year.

Budget people have often been isolated from policy-makers, and policy-makers from the budget process. There has been little rotation of personnel between budget-making and substantive policy-making positions. In-service training to acquaint each with the problems, interests, and needs of the other could be followed by an increasing exchange of personnel between agency budget shops and functional or regional bureaus, between the Bureau of the Budget and the various departments. If many budget people are "narrow" and interested only in "line item" figures in a budget, with little knowledge of the programs the "line item" makes possible, it is because their present jobs require nothing more. Broader and more able personnel will be drawn to budget positions as opportunities for personal growth and experience are expanded. If many policy-makers ignore budget considerations, then training and experience in budgeting will make them more conscious of the importance of the budget process to the successful implementation of American foreign policy.

Arthur Smithies in his book, *The Budgetary Processs in the United States*,[2] suggests one method for shortening and simplifying the budget process, a means of lifting congressional attention from petty administrative details to consideration of programs and purposes. In brief, he calls for an "administrative budget report," which would be a statement of *past* organizational unit costs—not a projection—together with a "program budget," which would show proposed costs of the major substantive activities planned by an agency. The administrative budget report would be used as a device to improve administrative management, while appropriations would be based upon the program budget. The report would be a more accurate device for administrative management than the projections included in the present administrative budget. Use of the program budget for appropriations, it is believed, would encourage more sophisticated thinking and staffing in the budgetary process. It would make possible a concentrated effort on the part of members of the appropriations committees to develop a thorough understanding of policies and programs. Smithies declares the time between the flash estimate and allot-

---

[2] For the best contemporary treatment of the budget process, see Arthur Smithies, *The Budgetary Process in the United States*, New York: McGraw-Hill Book Co., 1955.

ment for the first quarter of a fiscal year could be reduced to twelve months if this process were adopted.

So far as authorization and availability of funds for more than one year is concerned, many in the executive branch would be only too happy to accept such a change. The Congress hangs back, fearing a loss of congressional control over foreign affairs. Authorization for longer but limited periods of time would make possible longer-range planning of political and economic cooperation with other nations than is now possible on a hand-to-mouth basis. It would provide a degree of permanence for the foreign affairs programs and free the Foreign Affairs and the Foreign Relations Committees from the annual review treadmill which drains their energies from the proper consideration of major problems in the foreign affairs field on a selective basis. Opponents point out that this would leave the annual review to the appropriation committees, which are much less friendly to most programs. If the Smithies proposal were to be implemented, this opposing point would be negated, because the nature of consideration by the appropriation committees and the caliber of their personnel would be substantially changed.

Most funds authorized and appropriated for foreign affairs programs must be obligated during the fiscal year for which they are appropriated. Since many underdeveloped countries are slow in making administrative decisions, it is sometimes difficult to activate programs within a year. It is said that the necessity of obligating within one year weakens the American position in negotiation with foreign countries and makes for worse choices rather than better because of the crash nature of programming. Availability of funds for periods of more than one year would tend to reduce the control over agency programs not only of the Congress but also of the Bureau of the Budget and the President. Nonetheless, in view of the need for more effective long-range programming, it seems essential to relax the present one-year cycle to some extent, probably for somewhat longer periods, though seldom indefinite, according to the special exigencies of each activity.

The changes suggested in the budgetary field are not those

which can be easily accomplished by the people actively engaged in the budget process, even though they may recognize the need for alterations in the process and improved personnel. The problem involves both the executive and legislative branches and is of great complexity, requiring consideration and support in both branches as well as from the public. It is possible that a joint nonpartisan legislative-executive-public commission should be appointed by the President in cooperation with the Congress to conduct a thorough study of the budget process and the procedures of authorization and appropriation. Its recommendations should be given careful consideration by the executive and legislative branches. Piecemeal revisions at lower levels may be steps in the right direction but are unlikely to bring about the major adaptations which are required for modernizing the present archaic budget system.

The President: Leadership and Coordination

As increasingly competitive world conditions complicate the problems besetting American foreign policy-makers, the need for more effective Presidential leadership and coordination of the departments and agencies, with major responsibility for various aspects of foreign policy, is likely to become clear to all. Only the President among top national leaders is in a position to balance domestic and foreign policies, to weigh the conflicting claims of the various departments and agencies, to allocate national resources among competing policies and programs. Only he can bear the ultimate responsibility for insuring the proper orchestration of the many devices employed by the United States in the conduct of its affairs overseas. No single Cabinet member is able to play the keys with objectivity, for each, no matter how good his intentions, is a representative of his own particular aspect of foreign or domestic policy. The nature of the machinery through which the President attempts to exert leadership and to attain coordination of the departments and agencies, with their divergent and conflicting interests, is likely to determine the degree of success he will achieve.

In past years, the President's personal staff has been held to a bare minimum. If it were otherwise, it is possible that "junior clerks" in the Executive Office of the President could sometimes outweigh the judgments of Secretaries of great departments of the government. Indeed, in spite of the relatively small staff surrounding the President, this charge has occasionally been made. The departments and agencies, and their leaders, have usually tended to encourage decentralization and compartmentalization. Congress has gone along, because a divided executive branch enhances its own power. Each department has sought to hold on to its own prerogatives, to deal with its problems by itself or directly with the President, rather than throwing them into a common pot. There was and is much to be said for this approach of letting the specialists in various aspects of domestic and foreign policy run their own shows, without substantial interference by any staff arm of the President or by other departments of the government. But, there were and are drawbacks as well. Many problems cut across department lines. The President is either dependent upon advice from a single source, or *ad hoc* meetings of interested parties have to be set up on short notice so that the President can be apprised of different points of view before making a decision. Lack of regular coordination of the departments and the sporadic assumption of leadership by the President only when an emergency arose was not good enough in the past, is not the formal policy in the present, and would fall far short of meeting the delicate requirements of the future.

As the need for increased coordination has become apparent since World War II, the trend has been toward the establishment of inter-departmental committees, meeting at regular intervals and generating policy recommendations, rather than through a substantial strengthening of the personal staff of the President. The National Security Council and the Operations Coordinating Board are the best examples of such committees in the broader foreign affairs field. Other groups with more specialized duties, as their names imply, are the Council on Foreign Economic Policy, the National Advisory Council on International Monetary and

Financial Problems, and the Interagency Committee on Agricultural Surplus Disposal. Government by committee tends to breed accommodation and compromise, to encourage "weasel" verbiage, to bring before the President an agreed paper which all the departments can live with. Hard decisions are not necessarily made. Splits in view between the agencies are not always clearly delineated for the President to consider. To be sure, the small staffs of the National Security Council and the Operations Coordinating Board attempt to prevent the preparation of such bland products as the basis for the President's consideration. Some major splits are elevated through NSC channels for Presidential decision. Attempts are made to force the departments to bring problems before NSC groups. But, the NSC-OCB staffs are small and those of the departments so large that it is often an unequal battle. True, the President also has the Bureau of the Budget to assist him in the allocation of funds and in the coordination of legislation. But, the Director of the Bureau lacks the prestige of a department Secretary and is often over-ridden or by-passed in reality if not openly by pressures brought upon the President by department heads.

"A President is many men," one writer has said in commenting on the staffing of the Presidency. Yet, in fact, the President is only one man, incapable of performing his varied roles unless he is properly staffed. There have been suggestions that some official short of the President, possibly a Secretary of Foreign Affairs or a Deputy President for Foreign Affairs, should be delegated the responsibility for much of the coordination of foreign policy. This may eventually become a possibility and a necessity. In the meantime, some adjustment might usefully be made in the balance of power between the President and the departments. The most modest suggestion for strengthening the hand of the President would seem to be that of giving him a stronger personal staff in the Executive Office, particularly in the Bureau of the Budget and the National Security Council. An increased number of highly trained senior level civil servants on these staffs would enhance the prestige of the Director of the Bureau of the Budget and the Special Assistant to the President for National Security Affairs. It would make possible more effective Presidential leadership of the foreign affairs departments and agencies and greater coordination of them in planning and implementing American foreign policy.

LOOKING INTO THE FUTURE

It is difficult to foretell with complete exactitude the future role of the Department of State within the government-wide hierarchy of the foreign policy process. As previously pointed out, some have suggested that a Secretary of Foreign Affairs with a personal staff, somewhat similar to the present Secretary of Defense in relationship to the Army, Navy, and Air Force, should be established to coordinate the efforts of the Department of State, the International Cooperation Administration, and the United States Information Agency. These two super-Secretaries might be joined in the President's inner councils by Secretaries of Domestic Affairs and Financial Affairs, thus reducing to four the number of top-level department officials reporting directly to the President.

If this proposal at first sounds a little radical, it does deserve consideration. Such a step would be likely to reduce the number of representatives present in National Security Council discussions, fostering an easier exchange of views between the most interested parties. It might keep some minor matters, which now make demands upon his time, from reaching the President. Actually, so far as the Department of State is concerned, it would represent a downgrading—in the same sense that creation of the Department of Defense separated the Army, Navy, and Air Force from the President by a new level in the hierarchy.

A new Secretary of Foreign Affairs, however, could serve much the same function as the present Secretary of State. Even now, the International Cooperation Administration is subjected to a relatively detailed policy control by the Department of State, and the United States Information Agency receives policy guidance from the Department on a daily basis. The proposal to create four super-Secretaries is not a direct break with the past in the foreign affairs field but a further development of a trend already becoming obvious. It has been suggested that under such a reorganization the Secretary of Foreign Affairs, like the President, would remain most of the time in Washington and the continental United States, and that most high-level negotiation abroad would still be conducted by the Secretary of State. Whether this distinction would in fact be implemented or maintained remains to be seen. If it were, many would consider it an additional argument for the creation of a Secretary of Foreign Affairs.

From a psychological viewpoint, an alternative suggestion—that the title of Secretary of State (instead of Secretary of Foreign Affairs) should be accorded the proposed foreign affairs super-Secretary—has considerable merit. Serving under such a new-type Secretary of State, within a super Department of State, would be Secretaries of Foreign Affairs, Economic Affairs, and Information Affairs. The Secretary of Foreign Affairs and his Foreign Affairs Department would be responsible primarily for political affairs, with the present Department of State interests in economic and cultural affairs probably devolving upon the departments to be headed by the Secretaries of Economic and Information Affairs.

Whether one agrees with the proposal for a super-Secretary, be he called Secretary of Foreign Affairs or Secretary of State, one fact should stand clearly revealed. Adaptive change in the policy machine responsible for the formulation and implementation of foreign policy must continue if the United States—itself ever-changing in an evolving world situation—is to be successful in its search for survival during the next half century.

A creative adaptation of organization and policy to a world environment in flux is essential if America and Western civilization are to avert a decline similar to that of so many great nations and civilizations of the past. Possibly we will refuse to seize destiny by the hand in our brief moment of world leadership, and be pitched into the trashcan of history. Yet, with a recognition of the needs of the foreign policy machine and a vigorous effort to meet them, we can unlock the doors of the future and move forward with some confidence and hope toward the fulfillment of man's highest aspirations.

INDEX